The
Termination
Handbook

The Termination Handbook

Robert Coulson

 THE FREE PRESS
A Division of Macmillan Publishing Co., Inc.
NEW YORK

Collier Macmillan Publishers
LONDON

The Free Pesss
A Division of Macmillan Publishing Co., Inc.
866 Third Avenue, New York, N.Y. 10022

Collier Macmillan Canada, Ltd.

Library of Congress Catalog Card Number: 81-66988

Printed in the United States of America

printing number

3 4 5 6 7 8 9 10

Library of Congress Cataloging in Publication Data

Coulson, Robert.
    The termination handbook.

    Bibliography: p.
    Includes index.
    1. Employees, Dismissal of—Handbooks, manuals, etc.
I. Title.
HF5549.5.D55C68   658.3'13   81-66988
ISBN 0-02-906700-6   AACR2

Contents

Preface

WHY WOULD ANY ONE WRITE A BOOK about people being fired? Terminating an employee is a chore that most executives want to put behind them as quickly and as painlessly as possible.

Get someone else to do it. Better still, get the worker in and get him out. Get the problem out of the office.

Firings are not what most people like to think about or to talk about, certainly not something to be discussed with the workers.

Unfortunately, the subject cannot be ignored. Almost any employee may be discharged. In appropriate cases, managers are obligated to recommend termination, and supervisors must discharge workers. How people are fired is a crucial but somewhat secret area for American executives and employees. It is crucial because the termination-at-will doctrine places a weapon in management's hands. It is taboo because Americans like to think positively about themselves; no employee wants to feel powerless.

I wrote this book because it is needed. As president of the American Arbitration Association, I must review hundreds of discharge cases. Many managers and workers who are involved in employment terminations are floundering, ignorant of the legal rights of employers and employees, unaware that the rules are changing, insensitive to the trauma of losing a job. I have seen too many cases where people's careers have been blighted because of such miscalculations. Someone was discharged without cause; the executive who did the firing was held accountable. An employee who should have been terminated was kept on the job; morale in the office plummeted. A dispute over a termination found its way into court; both parties suffered.

The Termination Handbook is written for managers, for supervisors, and for workers. It tells how people are fired, how to fire people. It explains why people are fired and how the rules are changing. Anyone likely to become involved in a termination should take the time to read this book.

I am deeply grateful to the many arbitrators, attorneys, executives, and union representatives who have helped me in its preparation. This book represents my personal views, not necessarily theirs. Nor does it represent any policies of the American Arbitration Association, except to be impartial on this subject, as in others.

I would like to personally thank Paul A. Salvatore who assisted me with the research, Dorothy Hans my administrative assistant, and my associates on the staff of the American Arbitration Association for their excellent advice and broad knowledge of the field.

Sorry, You're Fired

THIS BOOK IS ABOUT PEOPLE being fired. It tells how people are given the Bad News. It is written for the employee who may be fired, but also for the supervisor who has been told to discharge a worker and for the manager who may have decided that the employee had to go.

You think that it can't happen to you. Be realistic. You know how the system works. New people are hired: older employees are let go. People are constantly losing their jobs. Are you exempt?

When you accepted your job or selected a career, you may have increased the risk unwittingly. In some fields, the danger of being fired is very great. Publishing, consumer advertising, managing a Rock group, football coaching, chief executive of a broadcasting network; these are some of the more insecure professions. As one woman explained:

> In the magazine business, we have what is commonly called a purge. I was hired by one manager. When he went, I went. I was the ad director. The new manager brought in his own people. These things happen. You've got to take them in stride. I'll find something soon.

Other careers are more secure. Some positions are eminently safe: librarian, public school teacher, municipal clerk, Justice of the Supreme Court of the United States. Some jobs are so secure that they become boring, so dull that their incumbents do everything they can think of to get fired. One young worker threw a custard pie at the company's consultant. He was fired.

You may think that your job is secure. Even a well-protected employee may be terminated unexpectedly, particularly when management changes. Some hard-nosed executive who has orders to reduce the overhead may be looking around for someone to dump. It can happen.

> The chairman of the board was changed. The change went right down the line. I was an administrative assistant to the head of marketing. His boss went. Then he went. Before he was fired—terminated they called it—he had warned me that he didn't know what would happen to me. Well, they merged domestic and international operations. My job sort of disappeared. They offered me a position as a typist. No way. So they fired me.

The man who fired her received his assignment from the head office. For several weeks, he prowled around, sacking one person after another. At five o'clock on a Friday afternoon, he walked up to her desk and said, "This is your last day." When she called in on Monday morning, the office manager told her that lack of work was the official reason. By then, she was off the payroll.

The prime-time nightmare for sixty million working Americans is to be called into the boss's office . . . and fired. Sometimes it is done diplomatically, at other times with needless cruelty.

One executive was told, at the end of his termination interview, that there was no need for him to go back to his office. All of his possessions had been taken from his desk and packed in a carton. He could pick them up at the reception desk. He went home, feeling like a thief.

Herman Melville's short story, *Bartleby,* offers a classic account of an American firing. Bartleby was a scrivener, someone in a lawyer's office who copied legal documents by hand. After working for the lawyer-narrator for several days, he was asked to help compare a copy with the original. His employer was surprised to hear him say, "I would prefer not to." Bartleby also refused to do other chores that fell to scriveners. Moreover, he took up residence in the lawyer's office. After several months, he even "preferred not" to copy documents.

The kindly lawyer was stumped. The time had come to discharge Bartleby.

> At length, necessities connected with my business tyrannized over all other considerations. Decently as I could, I told Bartleby that in six days' time he must unconditionally leave the office.

Six days passed, then the lawyer took action:

> I buttoned up my coat, balanced myself, advanced slowly towards him, touched his shoulder, and said, "The time has come; you must quit this place; I am sorry for you; here is money; but you must go."

Bartleby remained silent. The lawyer took an even firmer line. He ordered the man to leave, and went home for dinner. On the following day, Bartleby was still there.

> "Bartleby," said I, entering the office, with a quietly severe expression, "I am seriously displeased. I am pained, Bartleby. I had thought better of you . . . Will you, or will you not quit me?" I now demanded in a sudden passion, advancing close to him.

Bartleby replied that he would "prefer not" to leave. And so he stayed. What was the kind-hearted lawyer to do? What else but to vacate his office? Such an outcome may seem quaint and dated, since a modern employer would persevere. But Melville's dialogue is contemporary enough. Employers mumble the same way today when they discharge workers:

"I am sorry."

"Here is money."

"I am pained."

Employers still dislike firing workers, as they did then.

Being kicked out of a job provides the theme for many American novels, soap operas, and films. The fear of being fired touches a deep nerve. In our society, a person's job is crucial. We find our identity in our work. When we lose our job, we lose our character, our essence. We live in a free society, but most of us are afraid of being given our "freedom."

In America, people are not guaranteed a job. Our national unemployment rate fluctuates between five and ten percent, depending upon the economy. In our "free society," unemployed people are *free* not to work. Workers are *free* to change jobs. Employers are *free* to terminate workers.

Employees get laid off whenever operating expenses must be trimmed. They are canned in batches when business turns sour. Individual workers are terminated for good reasons, and sometimes for no reason at all.

Some employees are protected. Union members enjoy job security because of their collective bargaining contract. Government employees are sheltered by various civil service laws. But most American workers are subject to dismissal at the whim of their employer.

Many workers are afraid of being fired. Family income usually depends upon the salary. Bad things happen to workers who lose their jobs: alcoholism, chronic illness, and child abuse, among others. Prevention centers understand the connection between unemployment and suicide. Family life deteriorates for the out-of-work, mirroring a loss of purpose, a breakdown in self-value.

Audrey Freedman of The Conference Board, a business research service in New York City, explains why jobs are important: "Our only social cement is work. It sets our hours and relationships, and it structures our lives. It keeps us from coming unglued."

Pathological problems can result from losing a job. That kind of freedom can destroy a person. Stress-related diseases have been identified with job loss. Personality disorders often result from the firing itself.

The breakdown can be explosive. The *New York Times* told the story of a young man who lost his job at an automotive shop on Long Island, during the long, hot summer of 1980. He argued with his father at the breakfast table. Suddenly, he grabbed a knife, stabbed his father several times, bit his mother in the arm, and staggered out of the house. He jumped into a neighbor's car, couldn't get it started, tried another, and finally found one attached to a boat trailer that would work. He drove head-on into another automobile that was occupied by five people. All were injured. He jumped into still another car that had three children in the back seat. While their mother watched in horror, he drove off at more than seventy miles per hour, racing wildly around the neighborhood, finally plowing through a fence into some people waiting to buy hot dogs and soft drinks. He killed two children outright and shoved a man two hundred feet across the patio, pinning him against a cigarette machine, crushing him to death. More than a dozen people were injured. The badly injured, unemployed driver was pulled from the wrecked car and taken to Nassau County Medical Center in critical condition.

All for the loss of a job!

Certainly, most people who lose their jobs have less bizarre reactions, but deterioration in family and community relationships is common, accompanied by signs of general depression.

An article by Saul Friedman in the February 1976 issue of *The Progressive* describes the problem in stark terms. Quoting Greg Hilliher, a social worker in the County Welfare Department in Flint, Michigan:

> Unemployment is the primary reason for child abuse, without a doubt. The story has become so common it would be a cliché if it wasn't so terribly sad. A man has been employed for maybe ten years. He had a decent in-

come, a modest house, perhaps even a camper, and lot of payments. He had debts, sure, but he also had hope. Then came the layoff.

Many of the workers in Flint were covered by union benefits and by unemployment insurance. When these payments ran out and workers had not been called back, the pressure escalated. Hilliher describes a typical unemployed father:

> He lived by the skin of his teeth, even in good times, because there was always something to pay for. And now it gets worse and his optimism fades. He's around the house almost all day and he has fixed everything in sight. He sees the kids when they are dirty and noisy and misbehaving. They don't pay him the same attention they used to. He was the boss, the breadwinner. His relationship with his wife changes. He bosses her around because he has to prove that he's still the man of the house. He has to go to the welfare office or he's around the house when the welfare worker makes a call. In such a situation, everybody in the house gets bent out of shape. I don't know how many cases I've had where the father admits that what his kid did would normally not have been cause for a reprimand. Or it would be overlooked. In the house of the unemployed, there is so much tension that it's like striking a match in a room full of gas fumes. The child misbehaves, the father loses his temper and smacks much harder than he intended. Most of the child-beating cases that we have been seeing are discipline related. There is no attempt to hide what happened. The hospital shows me a child covered with bruises and when I ask the parents what happened, the father breaks down and tells me he did it. He says over and over again that he's sorry, that he simply lost control, that if he could only find a job he would make it up to the child.

Being fired initiates a time of stress. Mortality rates increase. People lose their confidence. Sometimes, they lose their will to live. For good reason, discharge is called the "death sentence" of industrial discipline. Modern times are already depressing enough for many Americans who are unable to cope with rampant inflation and struggling to keep their heads above water. When they lose their jobs, they lose everything.

When you have a job, you have a place to go. People at work know who you are and want to talk to you about the job. You answer your phone. You are plugged in. You have things to do. Each day, you have a place to go and people to see.

When you are fired, you have no place to go. You have no phone, no function. You reach out for friends, but find that they are busy and have no time for you. Suddenly, you know that you are a failure. Unemployment shatters the worker's self-image as a valuable, productive person.

Regardless of the reason for termination, even if the word is put out that you resigned voluntarily, the job is gone. A sense of despair is likely to set in. The reality of not working during a time of your life when you expect to work may be the cruelest aspect of our free society where no one is guaranteed a job. Most of us were educated and trained with a career in mind. Employment has become the key to our identity.

It has become difficult to switch jobs. Increasingly complex technology demands specialization. We are no longer generalists in a simple society. Jobs require extensive education and experience and involve skills that are not easily transferable.

Whether we are round pegs or square pegs or Harvard pegs, we are expected to find a place for ourselves in the working world. When we are plucked out and tossed into the bin of rejected people, "failure" may be the only tag that we can find for ourselves. In America, workers are free; free to sink or free to swim.

"No one is going to want me" is the credo of the discharged worker. A discharged employee may discover that it is difficult to find another position. Even where a good-hearted boss is willing to say that the former employee "resigned voluntarily and only to find a greater challenge," gossip may throw a roadblock across the path to new employment.

We live in a wired society. Information is transmitted quickly, usually to the detriment of those who are fired. The world's opinion is fixed by casual, wounding words that leave no trace. Unemployed people can become paranoid, suspecting that an evil conspiracy is at work to keep them from finding work. There is no conspiracy; it is simply the "system" operating.

Both workers and supervisors should try to understand that system. Employees who understand why people are fired can avoid becoming victims of the system. Sometimes employees leave an employer no choice but to fire them. It is possible not to be so stupid. In Chapter 3, the discipline and discharge system is explained: why people are fired and how such decisions are made.

It is cruel to discharge a worker unnecessarily. Very often, a worker can be saved; performance can be improved. Even where termination is justified, it should be done thoughtfully and reluctantly, with the least harm to the individual. An employer has an investment in each worker, one that should not be tossed aside casually. It is good business to care about people.

If an employee sues a former employer because the termination was unfair or carried out with cruelty, both parties may become losers. The worker will have embarked upon a costly, traumatic journey through the courts. The employer may shoulder much of the cost or be plagued by guilt. Win or lose, termination litigation is a drag.

The advertising and sales promotion director of the Burlington Draperies Division, Jean Spencer, was terminated in 1974 when her job was eliminated in an economy move. She was in her early fifties, with twenty-five years' experience in marketing and merchandising. While she looked for another position within the company, Spencer was allowed to occupy a spare office in the personnel department. During that time, she approached top executives in the company trying to find a line management position. The one position that was offered did not seem to lead to a line job.

Finally, the personnel department told her to vacate the office. She was out of work for a year and became depressed. She felt that her friends were avoiding her.

> It was a terrible situation. You're desperate, because your're afraid you can't pay the rent or manage. I was used to working. I've worked practically all my life. I've had a job since I was twelve years old.

She filed a sex discrimination charge with the New York Commission on Human Rights. In 1980, after a hearing, the Commission awarded Miss Spencer $273,387.09. Her claim was sustained in court. Burlington appealed the decision as exorbitant. Litigation in the courts may go on for years.

It is rare for parties to benefit from employee lawsuits. Both parties suffer while the case drags on. At the end, there may be no winner. There must be a better way to handle such problems.

American workers no longer expect to live with fear, but the fear of being fired is widespread. Young people are told that jobs can be a challenging source of accomplishment. They seek a decent place to work, a humane atmosphere. Job security should be an important part of the working environment.

Recently, I interviewed a Dartmouth graduate. "I am looking," he said, "for a job to which I can commit myself, with an institution that I can be proud of. I want to wrap myself around something that I can help build, that will become part of me, something really permanent. The big corporations hire people and use them, and then spit them out again. I am looking for a career." How many American employers want that kind of marriage?

Should it be more difficult for employers to fire a worker? The workplace has become the subject of many state and federal statutes. Some of these laws protect workers against dangerous work conditions or unfair treatment by an employer. The right to discharge workers is limited under other laws. Should every worker be protected against unjust discharge?

The threat of litigation, the fear of unions, and quality of working life considerations has already persuaded some managers that employees should be terminated only for good cause. Employees may expect that unfair terminations by a supervisor will be reviewed by management. For whatever reason, employees seem more secure in recent years. This may be a fool's paradise. A Gallup Survey in the *Wall Street Journal* on November 21, 1980, reported that 59 percent of the chief executives in large companies say that their managers are more likely to dismiss incompetent workers than they were a few years ago.

Federal and state equal employment laws are increasingly important. When they are involved, the employer had better be able to justify a termination. When a black worker is fired, or an expected promotion is denied to a woman, or an older executive is forced into retirement, warning bells should jangle in the personnel department and in the front office. These cases alert the attention of top management because, if these laws are violated, the corporation may be liable for substantial damages. Chief executives like to know about such problems. A board of directors does not appreciate messy litigation. Charges of job discrimination can become very messy.

Grievance systems within the corporation have the advantage of resolving such problems without publicity, without bringing them to the attention of enforcement agencies. This is "enlightened employee relations." The use of internal employee complaint systems has been growing.

While most employers are willing to listen to their employees' complaints, they still claim the right to terminate employees. The bottom line is that it is tough to be a manager. You have to be willing to get rid of people who can't do the work or who won't do the work.

In the absence of a protective statute, American courts deny that an employee has any general right of review when removed from a job. An employer can fire a worker, and unless the employee has been hired for a definite period of employment, the employer does not have to give any reason for the termination.

Where employment is under a contract, the employer must show that the employee failed to meet its terms. Courts have held that a discharge can be justified for negligence, incompetence, inefficiency, neglect of duty, disobedience, insolence, unfaithfulness to the employer's interests, unfitness, intoxication, dishonesty, or immoral, disreputable conduct. How many people want to contest such issues in court against their employer?

Most of us don't work under a contract. About 65% of all American employees work on an at will basis. We are unprotected. According to the legal textbooks, the most fundamental rule of the law of master and servant is that an employer enjoys an absolute power of dimissing an employee, with or without cause. But the law may be changing. It is important to know your rights when you are being fired or are firing someone else.

The Termination Handbook contains advice for people on both sides of the "firing" line. It is based upon my work as President of the American Arbitration Association, where I have become familiar with hundreds of discharge cases. It analyzes landmark court decisions, labor arbitration awards involving discharge for cause, and the rulings of unemployment insurance boards. It compares the American system of termination with how workers are treated in other countries.

Most important, it contains practical advice for people who must become involved in a firing. Whether you are a personnel officer, a line supervisor, a manager who must terminate an employee, or simply a worker who is likely to be fired, you should read this book. It may save your job. It may keep you from mistreating another human being.

If you are about to be involved in a firing, you should prepare yourself. This book can help you do so.

CHAPTER 1

Being Fired

Aᴍᴇʀɪᴄᴀ ʜᴀs ʙᴇᴄᴏᴍᴇ a land of big institutions and tiny people. Former chairman of Common Cause John W. Gardner put it very well: "In our vast, impersonal society it is all too common for citizens to feel anonymous and powerless."

Oh sure, many of us think that we control our own lives. We have a job. We have a circle of friends and a family. We have roots in the community, or we can rationalize that we don't need to be entangled. Our world seems secure.

But it is not so secure. When big institutions make a move, most of us don't have much to say about it. Our lives can be altered suddenly, without us understanding exactly what happened. This is particularly true when it comes to a job. Today, you are working. Tomorrow?

Henry Johnson was a supervisor in a big, successful New York insurance company. Business was good. Henry felt certain that his unit was operating efficiently. He went to the Wednesday morning executive staff meeting, feeling secure. He almost choked on his coffee when the personnel director passed the word that every department had to reduce payroll by 9.5 percent within one month. Operating costs had to be cut. "The cost ratios are out of line." Good God, thought Henry, that would mean at least five jobs from his department. Could he do it?

In Henry's department, John Knowles was completing a statistical report. John did careful, methodical work. John was fifty-seven years old and had been with the company for thirty-six years. His wife worked as a teller in a suburban bank. John liked his job, but John was expendable. Management wanted to make room for younger executives.

Friday morning:

"John, I have some bad news."

"What could be bad today, Henry? The weekend is upon us."

"We have to reduce the number of people in this department. I got the word from the top floor."

"I am sorry to hear that, Henry. Who is going to go? My group is shorthanded already."

"I am really sorry, John, but you are on the list."

"You can't be serious. You and I put this department together. This is my life. I know this operation better than anyone."

"John, if it were up to me, it wouldn't be you. It wouldn't be done this way. You are the best man I have in the department. But the decision has been made. At least you qualify for early retirement."

"Is that why I'm being dumped, because I'm older than the others? Are they trying to save a few bucks on my salary?"

"No. Well . . . maybe they need to make room for some of the young tigers."

"Where does that leave me?"

"Maybe you can find another job. You can count on me when it comes to references. I will go all out for you."

"My God, Henry, what can I tell my wife? I can't find another job at my age. How did you let this happen?"

"There was nothing I could do. They told me what I had to do. I have to do it."

Next on the list was Zora Sanchez. She was new with the company, a Cuban-American. Zora had been working in the department for only six months. She had an infant daughter. Her mother cared for the child during the day. It would not be easy for

Zora to find another job that paid as well. Henry beckoned her into his office.

"Miss Sanchez, I have been told that I will have to reduce the staff of my department by five positions. You have been selected as one of those to be released."

"Oh, I am so sorry, Mr. Johnson. To which department will I be assigned?"

"You don't understand. There is no place for you in the company. Every department is being reduced."

"Why is this happening? We are so busy. Just last week, you said that business was good for the company."

"I don't know. It has been decided. There was nothing that I could do. With your severance pay, you will have time to find another job."

"Oh, Mr. Johnson, I will never find such a good job. I was happy here. Is it that you do not like my work?"

"No. Zora, it had nothing to do with me. You are a good worker. We all like you. Unfortunately, you have been here the shortest time. Please go now to the personnel department to pick up your money. I am very sorry."

"Yesterday, one of the girls in the auditing department, a Puerto Rican woman, said that the Spanish people were being pushed out. Is that true? There are few of us working in the company. She wanted me to sign a paper."

"No, Zora. It's just that you are one of the newer employees. It has nothing to do with being Cuban."

"I wonder, Mr. Johnson. I wonder."

Henry went home that evening, sad and unhappy. He had failed to protect his people, not that he could have done anything to save them. The decision was made at a higher level. He did not understand. Why did it have to happen, he wondered.

Henry Johnson was a decent man. He was sorry for John and Zora and the others. He knew that they would have difficulty finding jobs. John was too old to make a fresh start. Zora would have trouble because of her English. He had done what he was told to do. Today, he had terminated five people. Tomorrow, someone might fire him. It seemed to Henry Johnson that the company no longer cared about its people.

Nobody ever told Henry Johnson how to fire people. Nobody tells most executives how to do it. They are trained to interview, to hire, and to supervise, but hardly ever are they trained how to discharge. Moreover, nobody tells them what to do when *they* are fired.

Advice for Someone About to Be Fired

There are many ways to be fired. None of them are pleasant. Being fired is Bad News. Often, the victim has no idea why it happened, can do nothing about it, and carries away a wound that never heals.

Every employee should look out for storm signals. It can happen to you. Be sensitive to subtle hints of trouble. If new assignments stop coming your way, if a promotion that you were counting on goes to someone else, if your boss no longer invites you to staff meetings, or if you receive a poor performance rating or are demoted, then face the music. Your prospects may be fading.

Watch peoples' eyes. Try to read their attitude toward you. Do they listen to you with respect? Or have they written you off? Is the boss thinking about getting rid of you? In little clues, you may glimpse your future.

If you decide that your job is in danger, you should analyze your feelings. Do you want out? Some people hate work. Or perhaps it is the particular job. The problems that have placed you in jeopardy may suggest that you are not satisfied with the work or with the environment. People seldom perform well in a job they don't like. Would you be happier somewhere else? Perhaps you should look for another slot. Don't cling to a job through lack of confidence, particularly when you are young and ripe with promise.

All too often, people remain in a position that they don't like and which does not suit their abilities until it is too late to change. Don't let yourself get trapped.

Don't expect to be warned. You may be called into your boss's office expecting a new assignment or even a promotion. He looks at you in a strange way. He can't seem to get started. Finally, he blurts it all out: you are fired and he is sorry.

Executives who must fire someone often are saturated with guilt. They proclaim their sorrow. Certainly, they are sorry for themselves, sorry that someone else couldn't be found to do their dirty work. Firing you is the last thing they want to be doing.

How should you react? Should you paste a false smile on your face, thank your boss, and head for the door? Should you start screaming insults? Should you collapse into a catatonic stupor?

None of the above!

If you are taken by surprise, you should ask why you are being terminated. Don't accept it. Request some time to respond. Don't let your boss nail down the terms. Make a date for later in the day or on the following day. The Big Discharge Poker Game is about to begin. Don't let the boss read your hand.

Many executives schedule firings on Friday afternoon, on the theory that the person being fired will be gone on the following Monday. As in *Arsenic and Old Lace,* the aim of the game is to get rid of the body. One expert claims that if your boss invites you to get together at an airport on Friday afternoon, you are doomed. Miss your plane.

One New York bank prefers to terminate executives while they are on vacation. One executive, returning from a camping trip with his family, received a call from the deputy director of his department, who lived in the neighborhood. He would come right over. The bad news was delivered on the doorstep, with the victim surrounded by sleeping bags, children, and knapsacks. He was relieved of his responsibilities and given two months to find a new job. Apparently, the department head couldn't face the task of telling the man himself.

Another executive returned from his summer vacation to find a memo on his desk transferring his duties to another person. He found another position in the same bank. Now, he anxiously calls his office whenever he takes a day off.

It is obvious why employers like to fire people who are away from the office. They hope that the termination will be accepted as a fait accompli. They hope that the employee will swallow the decision and never come back.

As the intended victim, it is in your interest to stall for time, to plan how best to play the termination game. You need to prepare yourself for negotiating the terms of surrender, your acquiescence to a severance arrangement.

First, examine the facts. Do you hold any high cards?

Finding Out Why

"What did they say when you were fired? Did they give any reason?"

"I don't know. They never said. I went into my boss's office to discuss the project that I have been working on. He gave a funny look."

"Did he say anything?"

"Not at first. Then he pushed aside the file that I had put on his desk. He stared at it for a while. Then he looked at me and said, 'Mary, you don't need to worry about this anymore. It will be somebody else's worry.' I was shocked."

This was a typical firing: no warning and precious little explanation afterwards. An employee is fortunate to receive a hint.

Let's say you hear a rumor. Now you need facts. Your investigation should be discreet. It may not be easy to obtain confidential, accurate information from other employees. Your co-workers are reluctant to offend you. They may not want to involve themselves in an unpleasant situation. You are already regarded as someone with a deadly disease, possibly catching.

Don't buy that theory. You are not necessarily at fault. Too many people think that being fired means that they are guilty of something. In most cases, people are fired for reasons that have little to do with their own work: It was the wrong job; business was bad; somebody didn't like them; management changed; the company was reorganized. Don't take it personally unless there is no other explanation. Life goes on.

Try to understand management's thinking, to see the problem through the eyes of your employer. As honest assessment is called for. Find out where you stand. Conversations with other employees and with members of management may give you some insight. Maybe your boss didn't like you, didn't want to work with you. Bad breath? Perhaps your performance was at fault.

More often, there wasn't enough work. The company had to cut back. That may be the easiest theory to accept because your ego is less involved. But why didn't they lay off someone else? Why you?

Don't do the guilt trip. The job is a single episode in your working life. In some businesses—advertising, publishing, sales—people expect to hop from place to place as they graze across the field. The important thing is to learn from each position. Learn about yourself and how you and your work were perceived by other people in the firm. Next time, you may avoid making the same mistakes. You may decide that you needed more training . . . or that you were not sensitive to peoples' feelings . . . or that you did not understand the requirements of the job. Try to learn from the experience.

Each worker makes a unique, personal voyage through the employment market. For some, a career offers a happy frolic with risk and opportunity. For others, it becomes a search for safe harbors where working life can unfold within a secure and tranquil haven.

Some executives are quite happy in an "up or out" environment. They are ambitious, competitive, hungry for challenges. They view office politics as an opportunity to play a brisk game of one-upmanship. If they become frustrated as they clamber up the corporate tree, they search elsewhere for opportunities. Those kinds of people don't mind being terminated if care is taken to respect their hungry egos. Opportunities may be greater some-where else.

Other workers are more interested in finding a permanent po-sition where they can develop their abilities, build a career, and establish themselves in a secure and productive setting. They are intent upon building their reputation and status. These people may resist being terminated. They "own" their positions and ex-pect to fill them for a lifetime. In a corporation where executives are expected to climb into the hierarchy, such people may be out of synch with their environment.

Attitudinal differences change as an individual moves through life. First, we tilt a lance at the dragons of ambition. Later, as family cares whisper caution, we tend to snuggle into a comfort-able job. At what stage are you?

It is easy enough for youthful achievers to exude raw con-fidence. Listen to jaunty, thirty-year old Jane Pauley, who re-placed Barbara Walters on the *Today* show, in a recent interview in *Quest 80:*

> I have no job security, you know. Nobody with a very good job does. So I'm on the line. Being Midwestern helps a lot. People tend to think that you're as stable as a rock; they doubt you'll be cut off at the knees tomorrow. I think there's something to that.

But another Midwesterner in his fifties, trying to sell stocks for a failing brokerage firm, does not express the same courage:

> Each year the pressure gets worse. I have lost my nerve. Too much seems to be riding on my job. When I think that I must prove myself over and over again to my customers and to the partners, I begin to sweat. I can't see going through this for many more years. It's all I know. What happens then?

If your working environment contains more stress than you can handle, you should start looking for a more secure position.

People will understand if you run for cover, a compromise that almost everyone makes at some stage in their career.

In some firms, the fear of being fired is as obvious and ugly as empty coffee cups. Everyone walks around worried. On Friday afternoon, people congratulate each other for surviving one more week. By Monday morning, some are missing.

Business may be bad. A tyrant may be shaking things up in an effort to weed out the deadwood. A power struggle in the front office may be poisoning the atmosphere. Whatever the reason, in that firm, nobody's job is safe. Everyone is insecure. The tension is so bad that people spend their lunch hours shagging jobs. If you work in such a place, figure out some way to go over the wall. If you have any influence in that kind of shop, try to improve the atmosphere. Find out what is wrong. Why are people feeling so miserably insecure?

A consultant may be able to help. Talking with the employees may disclose what needs to be done. Chronic anxiety is the wrong atmosphere for building a profitable business. In a small firm, the boss should take prompt action to improve the mood. In a larger organization, the problem may be more difficult to solve. Large corporations often have pockets of discontent, islands of insecurity. But something needs to be done, and quickly.

A corporation is a miniature society, governed by published rules and regulations. These documents are worth reading. If you work for a large company, you should become familiar with the setup. You should find out who is authorized to discharge employees and what kind of approval must be obtained before action can be taken. Find out if terminations are carried out in accordance with the book. Your own job might depend upon it.

You may discover some interesting arrangements. One company requires that no employee with ten or more years of service can be terminated until approval is obtained from the vice-president for personnel and from the chief executive officer. Until then, the employee must be carried on the payroll. That company is quite specific about what must be considered before someone can be terminated. To be certain that an employee has been treated fairly, every application to the chief executive must describe the employee's health, family circumstances, status of dependents, and financial condition. The separation allowance being recommended must be specified in the application.

Where long-term employees are fired because of unsatisfactory work, a reasonable period must have passed since the employee was placed on probation or given a final warning. Supervisors must have discussed unsatisfactory performance with the employee. A written record must be made, specifying corrective action. The employee gets a copy of this record. If the paperwork hasn't been done, the personnel department will not forward the recommendation to the chief executive. That CEO wants to know how long the unsatisfactory performance has continued, when the matter was discussed with the employee, what corrective measures were taken and whether any attempt has been made to relocate the employee in a less demanding job.

When an employee's job has been discontinued, the supervisor must show that he has tried to relocate the employee. This may involve bumping a junior worker. Or the employee may be placed in a less demanding post at a lower salary.

An exit interview is required to explore the employee's feelings and to explain why the action is being taken. The company tries to retain the employee's good will. In case of lay off, a generous separation allowance is provided, which is not available to employees who are discharged for misconduct.

Another company has a policy that no executive can be fired unless the supervisor has obtained approval from a higher executive level. By focusing two levels of management on such actions, the company tries to eliminate decisions based on personal feelings. The intent is to convince employees that job decisions are receiving thoughtful review from management. But this is not a fail-safe system. If top management is capricious in its judgment, the review procedure may not improve the climate. In some companies, the employees have more faith in their local manager than in the faceless people at headquarters.

Employees view top executives through a distant glass. The

"bosses" are seldom seen. They may seem unapproachable, mysterious. The face of management becomes distorted as it passes down through the hierarchy from one level to the next. "Do you know what I heard yesterday?" a supervisor will say to his assistant, "They expect this group to increase production by thirty percent. If we can't do it, they intend to subcontract the whole job." Imagine how that kind of statement gets translated to the employees!

Lower-level managers may try to establish themselves as the "good guys," posing as staunch defenders against rapacious top management. With such an image, how much value should a worker place on the fact that his supervisor's decision will be reviewed by the head of the division?

"Anyway," one factory worker told me, "the whole personnel manual is bullshit. The plant superintendent has one job, measured in dollars, not people. When he says that some worker is wasting company money, nobody is going to stop him from firing that guy. This plant is no different than any other place I've worked. The boss calls the tune. If I don't like what he does, I better start packing my tools, 'cause I'm through."

What is true in a factory may be perceived as true in an office. Who has the right to fire? You need to know where that authority resides. Sometimes power is shared or may shift from group to group as changes occur. An organizational chart may obscure the reality of management power. Be alert. Your job could depend upon your knowing who controls your destiny.

In the corporate world, the power to administer the organization, to give orders, to command, and to punish or pardon is held within a relatively small group of managers. The control of the organization will be shared within that circle. You should know how the system works, what is expected, who you must satisfy. Corporations are highly political. Actions are taken because of the opinions, feelings, and decisions of a few people. Power is invisible. It shifts from day to day, like the weather. Keep one eye on your job horizon.

A similar climate exists in government agencies, trade associations, religious institutions, and in the operative arms of a socialist government. In every case, control is in the hands of a managerial elite. If your future depends upon the decisions of such people, you need to know who has a hand on the controls.

While ultimate control may reside in a board of directors, most personnel decisions are made by management. The directors seldom become involved in the firing of anyone except a chief executive. The management group decides which employees must be terminated, and it must carry out those decisions.

Employees usually are fired by their boss, but not always. The initiative may bubble up from below. Employees sometimes fire the boss. The president of a small savings bank was terminated when all but three of the employees signed a letter to the board of directors calling for his dismissal. He was a nice man, they said, but he didn't know how to run the bank; he wouldn't accept advice. They listed several critical errors he had made during the year, showing exactly how each mistake had hurt the bank. The board had no choice. The employees provided convincing reasons for firing the president.

Sometimes the employees in a department or branch office will decide that their boss isn't doing the job. What should they do? I know of situations where groups of employees have forced a confrontation, calling for the early retirement of their boss, a failing executive. Management takes such situations seriously. Such a campaign can be risky for the employees. Management's initial reaction may be to support supervision. But, when the employees have the facts and are acting in the best interests of the organization, they may succeed. I have seen it happen.

When you alone are being threatened, you may decide that if one of you must go it should be your boss. This can be dangerous. A direct challenge may end badly. If other employees share your views, a meeting with them can help you develop a strategy. Be careful! A collective effort by employees can have serious repercussions. Employers react impulsively when they discover that secret meetings are being held. Management may conclude that you are conspiring against their interests, that you are a union organizer, a trouble maker.

What if your fears are not realistic? In fact, your job was not in danger. If you seem to be worried about being fired, your position may deteriorate. People stigmatize a frightened victim. One personnel director calls this the "wounded animal" syndrome. If you are fearful of being terminated, be careful whom you confide in.

Talking It Over with Your Boss

You may decide that you need to talk with someone. The best strategy may be to confront the problem directly: talk to your boss. Ask if there are problems. Discuss your job in terms of goals and objectives. If a final decision has not already been made, persuade your boss to think in terms of improving your performance. You may save your job.

Who Made the Decision to Fire the Worker?

It sounds so respectable to say that management has concluded that a certain employee must be terminated! What does it mean? Where was the decision made? This is vital information to the person being fired. Was a determination made by upper levels of management for policy reasons? Who told the supervisor to get rid of the employee? What were the reasons? Or did the supervisor decide on his own? In many organizations, nobody wants to be identified as the person responsible.

Sometimes an employee will never find out why he was discharged. As Stewart Weiner wrote in *Los Angeles* magazine, "Nobody in this town tells you why you have been shown the door unless you are caught red-handed in the till or red-faced in the washroom." Even your own boss may not know. The mysterious stranger who made the decision may want to remain incognito or may be afraid of you.

"Tell Jones to get rid of her."

Still, after investing a portion of your working life with the firm, you have a right to know why you are being fired. Try to worm it out of your boss. Remember that he is scared and would prefer that you just disappear. He may try to avoid talking about the subject. He will say almost anything to get off the hook, anything, that is, except "Oh forget it, show up for work on Monday."

An employee's first reaction to being fired may be to get angry. Before doing so, remind yourself that your boss is probably the first person that potential employers will approach for information about you and your abilities. Don't burn your bridges! An employee should persist in trying to find out the reasons for the termination, being as objective as possible. Personalities may or may not be involved in the decision. Perhaps the supervisor simply decided that the worker couldn't handle the job.

Confronting the Reluctant Boss

Managers frequently procrastinate. While they delay, their unhappiness is transmitted to everyone else in the unit, including the intended victim. This is typical. Some executives seem unable to act.

The head of one company would worry himself into a severe depression, losing sleep and blaming the other executives for his predicament. His managers knew that he was unable to fire anyone. They had to terminate people while he was on vacation. As one manager put it, "our president is no good at confrontation." He always arranged for someone else to fire people.

Being fired is an important event in your career. You have a right to talk to the person who made the decision. Don't be fobbed off on some flunky. An executive may try to force the action by simply announcing that you are being terminated, leaving the details to be worked out with the personnel director. He wants to get it done as quickly as possible. Don't let your boss do a "hit and run" on you. You have a right to be told what went wrong.

In America, being a "good guy" is part of the lifestyle. As an employee about to be fired, you are a leper. Your boss does not want to be identified with such a loser. Furthermore, the person who has to tell you the bad news may be afraid of you. What if you create a scene? What if you sue the company? What if you blame him?

A boss will hardly ever say that someone is being "fired." He will say that "it isn't working out." He may offer you "a chance to resign." He may "give you notice." As Henry Johnson told John Knowles, the company needed "to reduce the number of people . . . you are on the list." Zora Sanchez was "selected as one of those to be released." Even the victims hesitate to use that blunt and violent word, "fired." They have "lost their job." They are now "at liberty." They are "looking for a new connection."

Behind this semantic delicacy is the bald fact that no thinking person wants to be identified with such a brutal, destructive act. Being fired is being rejected in the most fundamental way. For some people, the impact can be so traumatic that they drop out of the working world, escaping into vocational hibernation.

One executive stumbled out of a Philadelphia office after being fired. Rather than face his family, the poor fellow caught a plane to Miami, where he went underground for two weeks until sheer boredom gave him the courage to tell his wife what had happened. She had been distraught. Another victim continued to commute to New York City from Westport, Connecticut, for the balance of his monthly commutation ticket, before admitting to his family that he had lost his job.

Don't do that. Face the music.

An employee who is discharged may feel guilty. As one woman put it: "When I was fired, I decided that I was a total failure. That seemed to confirm what I had always suspected: I was no good. Probably I didn't deserve my friends: maybe not even to live. I wallowed in it. It took weeks for me to recover."

You should not feel guilty. You didn't fire yourself. Or did you?

What to Do Now?

"I hate to have to tell you this, but tomorrow is your last day." Whatever words the boss may use, the message hits you in the face: you are fired, terminated, out.

If an employee decides to fight for the job, steps to motivate management to reverse the decision should be taken instantly. Try everything. Be persuasive. Plead. Take it to the head office. Go right to the top. Use the "open door" that the president has promised. Do it quickly. At once.

If you decide not to fight, don't meekly accept the arrangement and sign the forms. Try to improve the deal, sweeten the severance arrangement. The company wants you to agree to the termination. Your boss is not sure what will happen if you don't agree. Play that card!

What should a person being discharged try to obtain? Three important goals for the employee are time, money, and a good story for the future. The employer may have somewhat different aims. In most cases, a compromise can be worked out.

Hang in There

Stay on the payroll as long as you can. Maintain a continuing source of income. Also, it helps to be employed when you apply for a new position. The use of an office address and telephone while prospecting can be immensely reassuring. Potential employers like to hire people who are already employed. If you can operate for a few months from your former employer's office, you will have an advantage. You don't have to be there from nine to five. There are advantages in having a place to pick up mail, to receive telephone calls, and to prepare resumes.

Some employers are willing to give such privileges to executives they have terminated. Others feel that it is bad for morale to have people hanging around after they are fired. They don't want the gossip about who was at fault, whether the individual was treated fairly, and who else is in danger of being dumped.

"My rule is to get them off the premises," one office manager told me. "That is non-negotiable."

Some Talk about Money

An employee being terminated should try to negotiate a substantial severance allowance. A generous termination, whether paid as a lump sum or in installments, will help to maintain your standard of living during a difficult period. Avoid having to make drastic reductions in the family budget. Being unemployed is traumatic enough. A firing will strain any family. Try to arrange things so that family life is disrupted as little as possible.

"I had been working for the same company for twelve years. I didn't realize how much I had come to depend on the salary check. It was credited directly to my bank account. My wife paid my bills. The salary was automatic, like the water that came out of the taps at home. After I was fired, the money tap was turned off. Suddenly I learned how much I needed that income. Mary and I sat down together at the kitchen table, figuring how we could survive without my salary. She said that it better not be too long. That put me into a panic. I was out looking for work next morning."

His wife told the same story, "We took John's job for granted. He never talked about it. I never asked him how things were going. When he got fired, I discovered that both of us had expected the company to take care of us forever. Now, I know that nothing can be that secure."

Your Cover Story

Everyone should agree on a plausible and convincing reason for the employee having left the position. People are terminated for many reasons. Job applicants are always asked why they left their last job. They need an answer that does not reduce their value as a prospective employee.

A job applicant should be truthful about the reason for the termination. You are more likely to get it right. You will have to live with your story. You should be candid with your family and personal friends. You should be accurate with business associates and with potential employers. Tell the truth, but stress the positive side. Make it brief. Don't dwell on the past. Stress your future potential. Protect your reputation.

If you expect to continue working in the same field, with some of the same people, it is a mistake to gripe about your prior job or to criticize your former associates. After all, you did work there. If they were so bad, why did you stay? If you say positive things, your former boss will be more likely to give you a good recommendation. Play down any conflict. A new employer may conclude that if you couldn't get along with your former boss, you probably won't be able to get along with your new boss. If at all possible, make the change look like an upward step in a successful career.

It may be better to say that you resigned, rather than that you were fired. Many employers offer that option. An employer may believe that an employee will find it easier to resign, less jarring to the ego. It may help the employee get a new job.

To Resign or to Be Fired

Resigning is not always best for the employee. Sometimes a worker is better off to be fired. Check your elegibility for unemployment insurance. An employee who resigns may not be entitled to certain company benefits. Under a contributory savings investment plan, a participant who voluntarily resigns may not receive benefits that are based on the contributions of the employer. Investigate carefully before deciding whether to resign or be discharged. Make sure that the options are explained to you.

Usually, the personnel department will explain the situation. Forfeiting your rights to such benefits sometimes may be preferable in order to establish that you were not discharged. Evaluate the pros and cons.

The executive who fires you may not understand the firm's benefit program. Don't count on his having done his homework. His primary goal is to get rid of you. Sometimes negotiations are carried out in haste and under pressure. It may be prudent to ask that a representative of the personnel department attend the termination interview.

Company representatives often agree upon their roles in advance. One is there to terminate the employee; the other may be responsible for negotiating the terms. The representative of the personnel department may only be there to answer questions, making certain that information about the benefit program is explained to the individual being terminated.

You should be sure that the details of the severance agreement are clearly understood. Take notes so that misunderstandings will not arise later.

A person being terminated should ask the employer not to contest unemployment benefits. A discussion of unemployment insurance follows later.

References

Generally, an employer will agree to give good references for the employee's job search. You can help by preparing a resume. Your boss should read it and should agree to verify the facts if asked. By obtaining such a commitment, you may guard against your boss minimizing your background or job experience to potential employers.

You should find out which executives are likely to be approached for job references. It may be best to channel inquiries to a person who will say good things about you, one who can be relied upon to answer questions in a positive way.

Don't warn a prospective employer not to talk to an individual. If you indicate that you have an enemy, it will pique an employer's curiosity. People have an insatiable appetite for gossip. They will want to find out why that person does not like you.

Don't give up your cordial relationships with people in the firm. Your friends may give you good job leads. Ask them to keep you in mind. Consulting assignments may become available where disloyalty was not involved in the termination. As a former employee you may be eligible for temporary, part-time jobs. You may be a preferred candidate for new job openings, better positioned than outsiders. If nothing else, your former associates may be feeling guilty.

Time to Talk Turkey

Plan an agenda for the termination interview. Be sure that you enter the meeting with a positive attitude, not with a chip on your shoulder. Don't be tempted to commit employment suicide. You are not a kamikaze mission! You are there to protect your future.

Be careful not to give your boss any reason to act impulsively. Don't start an argument about whether you should have been fired. Don't harass the executive who is firing you. That person is already under stress and is likely to lash out at you.

Don't attack management. Don't blurt out your opinion that the firm has always been a rotten place to work. Even an employee who is being terminated is expected to show loyalty. If an employee threatens revenge, no help may be offered during what can be an exceedingly difficult time in that person's life.

The transition from trusted executive to hostile outsider can be surprisingly sudden. A trade association that was moving from New York City to Washington offered its employees three choices: they could make the move and be reimbursed for their expenses; they could stay with the organization until the moving date and receive a generous separation allowance; or they could take early retirement.

One of the senior executives was asked to handle the logistics. That would have required a move to Washington, in advance of the general relocation. He was given several weeks to decide. He did not want to move his family to Washington and explained his reasons in a letter to the president.

The president accepted the letter as a resignation. In a memo, he thanked the executive for "important contributions to our work" during some sixteen years of employment. He relieved the man of all duties, gave him the normal termination allowance and "every good wish for the future." By sending that one letter, a trusted executive became an outsider.

The executive was furious. He had expected to continue working for another seven months. He sued, claiming that the association's offer to its employees was a legal commitment. To defend itself, the association retained a New York lawyer.

The president of the association was examined under oath. After many months, the association filed a motion to dismiss the complaint. A judge denied the motion: certain issues would have to be tried in court. The association appealed. The decision was affirmed by the Appellate Division. The case was placed on the trial calendar some three years after the termination took place. At that point, the lawyers were able to settle for a fraction of the original claim.

Litigation often delays the resolution of such problems. In the meantime, it destroys the possibility of friendly and productive relationships. In most cases, an employee would benefit from a prompt settlement. The best way to settle such a case is quickly, preferably at the termination interview.

Help from a Friendly Neutral

Third parties can assist in termination discussions. In the case I just described, one of the association's trustees might have been able to avoid the bad feelings and the expense of litigation by mediating the dispute.

If you are about to be fired, you should decide whether it would be prudent to bring a third person into the negotiations, perhaps someone with influence within the company. The person being fired may find it difficult to suggest such a thing. Injecting an outsider is not always easy. If the manager handling the situation feels threatened, some resistance may be expected. A less generous settlement may result. The success of such a ploy will depend upon who the third person is and how the suggestion is initiated.

In one case, a professional being terminated by a nonprofit agency asked a member of the board of directors to participate in the discussions. The employee and the director were black females. The intervention of the director probably avoided a messy and expensive discrimination claim against the agency. It also led to a generous severance arrangement for the employee.

The Bargaining Atmosphere

Termination agreements usually are negotiated directly between the employee and an executive. Treat that meeting like a poker game, an adversarial encounter. Past relationships between the individuals involved count for very little. After the decision to terminate has been made, the employee will be viewed as an outsider. Each side should recognize that a degree of hypocrisy is likely to pervade the discussions. The executive is responsible for getting rid of the employee and may seem pleasant, but behind the mask must lurk an unsmiling, business purpose.

"I feel like such a fink when people are being fired," one personnel director told me. "The department head is trying to ease the employee out, with the least possible cost against the budget. I understand that. The employee sits there, blinking away because his feelings have been hurt. I'm expected to sell him on the fairness of the company's severance offer. If he put up a fight, we would give him more. My job is to help the line manager get rid of him."

I asked him whether he enjoyed his job. "Not that part of it. I keep wanting to help the chumps who are being pushed out. They are perfectly decent people. In our business, we look for winners. When someone's time comes to be terminated, he doesn't know whether to be angry or hurt. I am the hearty salesman who persuades him to go along with the deal. Sometimes, it looks like a raw deal to me."

Victim or not, an employee should maintain a friendly demeanor, masking any bitterness. A person being fired is bound to feel resentful. Why not? The company seems to hold all the cards. It has had an opportunity to accumulate information about the worker: performance records, time sheets, disciplinary reports. If the discharge is based upon a particular incident, the company has been able to gather the facts, obtain statements from any witnesses. It has the employee's personnel file. It is familiar with the employee's character and personality.

If the termination is based upon a budget cutback or reduction in force, the company has the financial and operating data justifying the action. It has expert witnesses who will be able to explain the situation.

Employers have a common-law right to terminate without cause. If they need to justify a termination, they can select grounds that can be demonstrated. Moreover, the company has the power to grant liberal severance payments in appropriate cases. Most important, management representives can either help the worker find another job or can blacklist someone they decide to punish.

In court, employers can afford to defend themselves against an individual. They can hire a competent lawyer. They can delay the litigation, making it expensive and difficult for the plaintiff. The company seems to hold all the cards. Why should they bother to negotiate with any employee?

But an employee is not entirely powerless. If a worker is treated unfairly, the employer's public reputation and morale within the firm may suffer. If a termination is not handled in accordance with company policy, the responsible manager may be criticized. An employee may have friends within the company who will take an interest in the case, not to mention outsiders with influence within management ranks. An unfair discharge can be a rallying cry for unionization, for a class action, for a wave of employee discontent.

If some statutory right of the employee has been violated, the employee can play another card. Almost every worker is a member of some class that is protected by law. An increasing number of statutes have been passed to protect the rights of workers. A lawsuit may succeed under emerging theories of unjust discharge or violation of an implied contract.

Employers do not like to be sued. It is embarrassing, particularly for an executive who may have to justify the termination or explain how the situation arose. Managers want to avoid disagreeable squabbles after they fire a worker. That puts one more card in the employee's hand.

The Outplacement Consultant

Some corporations use outplacement firms to assist employees in obtaining new positions. These firms offer professional assistance to executives being terminated. They help them to find new employment, either within the corporation or with another employer.

Sometimes an employer will give the employee a choice: use the outplacement service or accept a cash allowance. Don't be too quick to take the money. The outplacement firm is hired to deal with the problems of the executive being terminated. It also serves to comfort the corporate official who has the thankless chore of discharging an employee. Outplacement firms can be retained for a particular individual or for a group of employees who are being terminated. Their services tend to be restricted to executives.

The outplacement consultant works closely with the executive who will handle the firing. During an initial conference, the problem will be discussed and the scenario for the exit interview will be planned. The background of the person being terminated will be reviewed. The consultant needs to know about the physical and mental health of that person. Family relationships will be explored. The consultant will have to strengthen the individual's self-confidence after he is terminated.

He will want to know why the person is being terminated. A plausible reason needs to be found that will not reflect upon the ability of the employee. The story has to stand up to scrutiny. It should leave the individual with as much self-respect as possible. It should not prejudice efforts to find a new job.

As soon as an executive is terminated, an interview is arranged with the consultant. This is a critical meeting. Most of the mistakes made by people who are fired occur within the first few days. It is important for a job candidate to start off on the right foot, with a positive attitude toward finding another job. Often, the consultant's first task is to convince the individual not to question the termination or attempt to get the employer to back down. The consultant will defend the decision, knowing that nothing will be accomplished by dwelling on the past.

From the beginning, the goal of the consultant is to rebuild the candidate's confidence toward obtaining another job. It is up to the individual, however, to find a job. As one consultant put it, "We are the coach. The candidate is the player. We develop the strategy. He carries the ball."

For blue-collar workers, other firms provide group counseling and job fairs. According to the *Wall Street Journal,* many major corporations such as Goodyear, Firestone, Jones Laughlin, and

Colonial Penn have used job counseling firms for blue-collar workers during periods of layoffs.

How about the Folks at Home?

The consultant will tell the individual how to discuss the problem with others. Candidates are advised to share their problems with their families and close personal friends who have an investment in the candidate's career.

"If you respect them, you should trust them to participate in dealing with your personal crisis." Don't try to hide the problem from your spouse. Talk it over together, quietly, objectively, and honestly. Decide what to tell the children. Don't underestimate their ability to understand. When in doubt, tell them. They deserve to be part of the solution.

If parents are honest, their families will be able to cope with the situation. Children have their own lives to manage, their own concerns. You should explain why money will be tight until you find a new job. Don't give your children the idea that this is the end of your world. Simply tell them that your career is in transition. They will understand.

As the weeks pass, and your efforts to get a new job do not click and your debts begin to accumulate, family pressures will mount. New problems will surface. It is good to talk about them. Otherwise, it is common for family members to stop communicating, to begin to fight.

"My wife began to get edgy after the first two months. I knew what was bothering her. She was still working, but would come home tired and nervous. Since I had nothing to do, I began fixing up the house: but nothing satisfied her. We came close to breaking up during that period. The money problem was getting her down. I was irritable because I wasn't making any progress. When I finally nailed down my new job, her headaches and anxieties cleared up. Thank God, it's over."

The children will also be feeling the stress. "My son seemed to lose his respect for me when I lost my job. Before, when I told him to do something, he would obey me. When he saw that I couldn't bring money into the family, he stopped paying attention to what I said. That really hurt. During the three months that I was out of work, I lost my son."

Getting That Next Job

The task of the outplacement consultant is to help the candidate find a new job by carrying out a methodical campaign. The consultant also tries to give the candidate renewed feelings of self-value.

Some firms ask the candidate to prepare a resume oriented toward achievements. They will explain the job search process, encouraging the candidate to regard it as a business assignment that requires careful planning and the use of successful marketing techniques. When job offers begin to arrive, the consultant continues to offer advice.

In many cases, the employee finds a new position, sometimes at a higher salary. Most executives find jobs within six months of their termination. For them, the problems of termination has been resolved.

The fee for the outplacement service is often a percentage of the executive's salary. Also, the executive may be kept on salary during the job search. Bridging pay is recommended, in preference to a single severance payment. Receiving a lump sum at the time of termination may reduce the employee's incentive to look for a new job. He may be tempted to take a long vacation. That can be a mistake. The longer you are out of work, the harder it is to get a new job.

When the executive gets a job, the bridging pay ends. Thus, the former employer has a financial stake in the success of the job search. A good reference from the former employer can be a vital factor in obtaining a position. If the consultant can assure that good things are said about the candidate by the client corporation, the likelihood of a successful job search will be strengthened.

Back to the Bargaining Table

It would be nice if every termination could be arranged in a friendly fashion, with the victim receiving help from an outplacement consultant and obtaining a new position at an even higher salary. Unfortunately, it sometimes rains on Monday. Some employees must haggle with their former employers over the terms of the separation.

If hard bargaining is anticipated, the person being fired should review the current financial needs of the family and personal priorities, and develop a strategy, just as one would in any other negotiation. You should look for ways to influence the outcome in your favor.

What are some of the power levers that are available to an employee whose head is on the block? Friends in top management can be useful. If a director or top executive is a personal friend and would intercede, arrangements are more likely to be harmonious and fair. A friendship with a major customer or with a community leader may have a good effect.

The business press sometimes contains stories about executives who have been fired by major corporations. Is there a public interest in your situation? A harmonious severance arrangement may be better for the firm's image than a messy, publicized squabble. If so, an executive's willingness to go quietly, without rocking the corporate boat, can provide an additional bargaining chip.

Great delicacy must be exercised about seeming to threaten an employer. Such a threat can convert a conciliatory atmosphere into one that is defensive and legalistic. Managers resent being threatened, particularly by assertions that a claim may be filed with a government agency. Executives don't like being bullied. An employee who talks about civil rights is on thin ice. The matter may be turned over to the company attorney.

An employee who is being fired may want to consult a lawyer. Select one carefully. Most lawyers are not experts on employee rights. Some attorneys specialize in litigation under the various employee protection laws. A few claim to have actions pending against hundreds of corporations.

For an older worker, losing a job can be particularly traumatic. Employees over forty are protected by the Federal Age Discrimination in Employment Act, which was passed in 1967. That law is quite clear: "It shall be unlawful for an employer . . . to discharge any individual . . . because of the individual's age."

In 1978, the U.S. Department of Labor processed over five thousand age discrimination claims involving employment. Each year, that number increases as older workers learn about the law and how to protect themselves. With high levels of inflation, early retirement at a fixed income is less attractive. When older workers are pushed out, many of them fight back.

"I can understand why the company wanted to get rid of me. I wasn't as flashy as some of the younger salesmen. But I knew the territory. I knew the product line. I wasn't the highest producer but I was pulling my own weight. It was when I had trouble with my back that they began to talk to me about early retirement. Once they got that idea in their heads, they kept after me and after me. They convinced themselves. OK. They fired me. But I don't think it's fair. I'm going to get them."

That man filed a claim with the Department of Labor. A sixty-four-year-old executive with Ebasco Systems, a nuclear engineering firm, was invited to take early retirement after fourteen years' service with the company. When he refused, he was terminated in October, 1978. After a trial, a jury awarded him $800,000. In May, 1980, a district court judge reduced the amount to $250,000. The company appealed the decision.

Corporations have learned to handle discrimination claims with care. The financial exposure has become significant. Not only can an employer be forced to pay damages to an individual plaintiff, but a class action may be filed on behalf of others in the same category.

Age is one of the statutory grounds available for testing terminations. Race, sex, and veteran's status are covered by similar laws. Religion is another catagory. In some states, it is illegal to fire an employee because he is an alcoholic, because that is considered a disease. The handicapped worker is protected by both federal and state laws. These and other emerging theories of liability will be discussed later.

It has become common for discharged workers to use discrimination as a lever for obtaining a better settlement from their former employer. In 1978, the New York State Division of Human Rights handled over two thousand discrimination claims alleging unfair dismissals.

The basis of a complaint to the government must be described as illegal discrimination. In many cases, an employee will have no difficulty devising some theory of discrimination. Women and minorities often claim harassment, as did one airline clerk. She claimed that her discharge for filing false payroll records was initiated by her male supervisor because he had asked for a date and been refused.

In offices where employees see each other socially after hours, embarassing allegations may come to light long after someone is fired. "My boss seemed to respect me, until the Christmas party. If I hadn't told him to keep his hands to himself, I never would have had this problem. After that, I couldn't do anything right. He has been picking on me ever since. Now, he has persuaded them to fire me. It isn't fair."

People who file complaints with the Division for Human Rights may not even want their jobs back. They want to punish the employer. In some cases, they expect to force a financial settlement. Companies take such complaints seriously. Even where a discrimination claim seems specious, the employer may worry that a major class action will evolve.

Complaints can be filed with an equal opportunity agency. Local agencies have various titles: fair employment practices, human relations or civil rights commissions. Most states and many local communities have created such agencies. They are monitored by a federal agency, the Equal Employment Opportunity Commission (EEOC). The EEOC itself receives over eighty thousand cases each year. Each claim results in a hearing where the employee has an opportunity to confront the employer. A settlement may result at that stage. Or the agency may rule that there is "no probable cause" for the claim. If the employer refuses to settle, the agency may issue a "right to sue" letter.

That is only the beginning. In order to use the courts, an employee must hire his own attorney and file a law suit. Most claims are dropped at that point. The court process is lengthy, expensive, and troublesome. Most people decide to devote their attention to finding a new job.

"I was mad as hell when I was fired. They had asked me to train a young man as my assistant. I took him under my wing, introduced him to the clients and taught him the advertising business. They had the gall to come to me and say that the budget would not cover both of us. One of us had to go. Me. I am certain that it happened because I was a woman. The department head was a flit. My assitant was one of his proteges. I took it to the chairman. He gave me twelve minutes of sympathy. Then I talked to the State Division of Human Rights. The company was stonewalling. When it came time to sue, I dropped it. I didn't want to ruin my reputation in the business. That turned out to be the right move: I got a job with another agency. The company didn't blacklist me. They could have. Maybe the chairman put out the word."

A Veiled Threat May Lead to a Better Offer

Corporate employers don't like to be sued. To avoid it, they may offer a generous retirement arrangement or a substantial severance allowance. As a practical matter, neither party should be eager to go to court.

Employers have adopted an increasingly conciliatory attitude, particularly where a claim can be settled quickly. Personnel directors have learned to evaluate such claims for what they often are, attempts to gain additional compensation. With experience has come sophistication.

An employee being terminated can often bargain for more money. A manager may have some discretion as to how much money can be paid. Not always. Some firms impose a strict schedule of termination benefits.

With new sensitivity to the financial risks of violating the discrimination laws, employers seem willing to put more chips on the table. The unstated fear is that an unhappy employee will complain to an equal employment agency or be the catalyst for an expensive class action. Where a member of a protected class is involved, these laws make it possible to bargain creatively.

At the exit interview, the company may be represented by a line executive or someone from the personnel department. They will be under pressure to bring the situation to a successful conclusion. They don't like the exposure, which can work to the employee's advantage.

If the person being discharged is able to set the correct tone, it may be possible to expand upon the employer's initial offer. This requires ability to make use of effective bargaining techniques. How are your negotiating skills? If you have a little time, there are some excellent books on the subject. Some research may be in order.

The Closing

The termination meeting is critical because once an employee has accepted the fact of being discharged, there may be no further opportunity to negotiate. When the exit interview is concluded, the employer will expect the deal to be buttoned up. Whatever pressure is available should be applied during that meeting. If you are successful, be sure that you have settlement. Don't rely upon vague promises. This is most important for the employee.

Notes should be taken, stipulating exactly what the termination benefits will be. Here are some important items that are sometimes overlooked:

1. You are entitled to whatever vacation pay you have coming. Insist upon receiving it. How about overtime, unused sick pay, compensatory time, or pay in lieu of notice?

2. Don't forget to compute the benefits that you may be entitled to under the pension or profit-sharing plan. Since the passage of the Employment Retirement Income Security Act (ERISA) in 1974, employers must follow the exact requirements of their employee benefit plans. There are heavy penalties for failing to do so. Be sure that you know your rights.

3. How long will you be covered by your company health insurance policy? Some plans contain a grace period. Get copies of the policies. How about your group life insurance?

4. If your spouse is working, find out if that health policy also covers you. Sometimes you can bargain for some additional time on the payroll to protect yourself against being left without major medical coverage.

The company should provide you with accurate information about the company's benefit program. Make sure that all the loose ends are taken care of: charge cards, company car, your personal possessions. Make a checklist of everything that you can think of.

Unemployment Insurance

A final thought for the discharged worker. The law provides a safety net for employees who lose their jobs called unemployment insurance. It is a vital part of the American system. A worker who is terminated should not hesitate to apply for benefits. Your employer paid for the insurance. You have a right to get some of it back. It is not charity. Look upon it as a return on investment. You are entitled to your share.

Go at once to the state office to register for your benefits and interview with a State Employment Service counselor. There are forms to be filed. If you were terminated, you probably qualify for benefits.

If your employer contests your claim, qualifying for unemployment insurance can turn into a hassle, with hearings before various state tribunals. The employer's contribution depends upon an experience rating, how many employees it has discharged into the fund. The employer may contest your claim to protect its rating. The state must satisfy itself that the employee did not leave on his own volition or was not fired for misconduct such as stealing, drinking, or violence. At first, your right to benefits may be denied. A claimant ultimately may win the case but since the process can be expensive and time consuming, it may be easier for you to get the employer to agree in advance not to contest the claim.

When you are notified that you are eligible, you will have to report to the unemployment office each week. Don't let it get you down. Millions of American workers go through the same experience. Your visits to the state unemployment office will reinforce your desire to go back to work. It is a depressing and dehumanizing place. Perhaps it is intended to be.

Unemployment insurance brings together people from all segments of our labor force. Blue collar, clerical, and professional workers gather there to collect their weekly benefit check. For some, the weekly trip to the unemployment office is the major event in their lives, because unemployed people live in a back eddy. Employed workers build their lives around their job schedule. When they lose their job, they float in an unregimented existence, supported by unemployment benefits.

The fund comes in handy for paid vacations for musicians, actors or other workers with temporary jobs. Or it can be used to supplement off-the-books compensation. The formal employment system in America is superimposed on a shadow employment market where payment is made in cash, not counted in government employment statistics. Off-the-books employment accounts for more than 10 percent of total wage compensation.

Almost everyone on unemployment insurance supplements the benefits with odd jobs or part-time work. Sometimes unreported income becomes their main source of support: unemployment compensation provides the supplement. Dealing in drugs or other illegal activities may generate more cash income than the unemployed person received from their prior job. But, mostly, it's just a question of working for cash.

Comments by unemployed workers reflect that shadow world as well as the formal system of employment:

I'm an actor, so I'm periodically unemployed. It's a regular rhythm in an actor's life. You never throw away your unemployment book. That's just the way it is; it's the federal government's subsidy of the arts.

I worked as a saleswomen for a large ad agency. One day my boss came up and told me that I would not be paid on salary anymore. All the salespeople would be on commission from now on, he said. I told him I didn't like the arrangement. He told me to take it or leave it. No job. I thought I could get work easily, but it is a lot harder than I thought.

I was a window designer. My boss wanted to pay me off the books after I had been with him for about six months. At first, I didn't mind. Money is money. It was kind of nice to be paid in cash. But I thought about it and told some of my friends about it and decided it was dishonest. When my boss wouldn't put me back on the payroll, I was through.

I am a bookseller. My ex-boss was the owner's daughter. She didn't know anything about the business.

We fought over how to run the shop. When we got into a big argument, she said that I'd better listen to her or she'd fire me. She fired me.

The fact is that I don't like to work. I am quite content doing nothing. As soon as I build up enough benefits, I always arrange to get fired. Then, I live with my family and take a vacation. What's wrong with that?

I'm trained to be a lighting designer. I couldn't find a job in design for a long time so I worked construction on a cash basis. Paid by the day. Odd jobs. I've got a job now as a designer. It starts in September, so I'm taking a paid vacation, compliments of Uncle Sam.

I worked as a salesperson in the garment district. My boss was an alcoholic. He used to go on tirades in the office, screaming and yelling at anybody or anything. One day, I was his target. Who needs it? I quit. I'll tell you though, the job market's a lot tougher than I thought. I even have played with the idea of asking for my job back.

A friend of mine bought a franchise in one of those chain store operations. He hired me as his manager. Things worked out great. We had our run-of-the-mill problems, but on the whole, things were o.k. One day he calls me on the phone at the store and says he's coming over. He called me aside when he got there and told me he was selling the store and moving out West. Marriage problems I think. Left me holding the bag. I had twelve employees to deal with. What a loser.

These comments by people on unemployment insurance illustrate how many different ways there are to lose a job. Some people quit. Others are laid off. Many workers are fired. In the third chapter, I will describe some of the reasons that employees are terminated. But before we go into that, let's talk about the right way to fire an employee.

CHAPTER 2

How to Fire
an Employee

THIS CHAPTER CONTAINS ADVICE for the manager who must terminate someone. Of course, even if you are the one being fired, you need to understand what is going through the boss's mind. You can be sure that there will be a strategy. The firing transaction is deadly serious. But like a game, it has rules and goals. There are fundamental guidelines that should be followed by the executive who must do the firing.

Preparation. A termination is an important management event. It should be preceded by careful fact gathering, analysis, and decision making, with the personal participation of those executives whose judgment should be involved. The final decision can be made by the boss, but other responsible executives should concur with the decision to terminate. There should be no second-guessing afterward.

"If anybody had asked me, I would have told them it was a mistake to fire Harry. Didn't they know he was old man Smith's roommate at Princeton? No wonder we lost our contract with Smith Machinery. Sometimes, I think the head office doesn't know what's going on."

Explanation. The logic of the termination should be explored and justified in advance of the final interview. If the individual is being discharged for budgetary reasons, financial data should demonstrate why the company must take such a step. Employees may appreciate the business necessity of employee cutbacks, but they expect the employer to have done its homework.

If an employee is being fired for poor performance, the record should justify the action. Often, the personnel director functions as a monitor, playing the role of devil's advocate with the line manager.

If management can demonstrate that a termination has been based upon a careful review and represents a consensus of the management group, the employee is more likely to accept the decision. No one likes to be treated casually.

The explanation to the employee must show that the decision was inevitable. It should demonstrate the reason for the action and explain why there was no acceptable alternative. Often it is helpful for executives to prepare for such an interview by role playing the dialogue in advance. One person should ask the hard questions; the other should try to provide impregnable answers. You had better be sure that you have the legal right to terminate the employee. If you turn out to be wrong, you could find yourself in big trouble. And the law is no longer necessarily on your side, as you will see in Chapter 4.

Finality. The goal of the termination interview is to convince the employee that the action is justifiable. With careful preparation, a united management front and an effective presentation, such a result is likely. In any case, management should stress that the decision is final.

Often, the employee will try to escape the inevitable, proposing alternatives that would postpone the final decision or asking for a further review. He must be turned away from such exits. Unless the employee believes that the decision is final, it will be difficult for him to deal with his own future. A "conversion" must take place. The purpose of the final interview is to convince the individual of the reality of the discharge, to get him to accept it as a fact as a change in status.

Even in cases where the reasons for the termination are difficult to justify, the goal of the company representative should be to persuade the employee to accept the fact that the company's decision is final. If the person being fired is left with any hope that the decision may be reversed, the meeting will have failed. As time passes, as that false expectation slowly fades from the person's mind, an inevitable bitterness may lead to a desire to punish the company.

When the former employee is convinced that there is no possibility of reversing the decision, the terms of the separation should be discussed. An employer should not try to bid for the employee's acquiescence to being fired. First discharge the person, then dicker over the terms. More on that later.

How to Fire an Employee

There are many ways to fire people:

- in a cold rage: over some seemingly incredible blunder
- sheepishly: the boss who apologizes for no longer being able to afford an employee
- mechanically: after following a measured sequence of progressive discipline, based upon the employee's failure to abide by the rules
- emotionally: the neurotic manager who tearfully tells a former confidant that irreconcilable differences have made it impossible for them to work together
- illegally: based upon race, sex, age, or some other invalid criterion
- sympathetically: with sincere, positive references to help the employee reach a higher rung on the ladder of success.

There are many ways to fire people. Many leave marks on the victim. For example, a rather bizarre firing involved a boss who decided to call it quits and fired his entire company. One of his executives, cast adrift suddenly and unexpectedly, told the story:

The owner of the firm, a private ad agency, called everyone to a meeting one Thursday morning. Nobody knew what the meeting was about. He announced that he was closing the business. He said it was the most difficult thing he had ever done during his entire business career, but he had decided not to work any more. He was tired of the rat race.

I was the marketing executive, responsible for about $8 million dollars a year in accounts. I worked closely with the owner, on a daily basis. He gave me no warning. He had notified the clients, telling them that he was closing their accounts. That killed any chance we might have had of buying the business from him.

When he announced it, there was total silence in the room. Nobody talked. Nobody moved. I had a lunch date scheduled for that day. I said to myself I could cancel and go back to my office and pout, or go to lunch. So I went to lunch. No severance pay was given. The president said there wasn't enough money.

As a footnote, he ended up dying of cancer about two months later. In my mind, that doesn't justify his disregard for the people that were his employees.

A more typical firing is described by a magazine editor:

While I was away on a business trip, the editor-in-chief, who had hired me, was asked to resign. Half an hour after returning, I was called into the president's office. He didn't waffle at all. He said, "I am going to have to fire you." He gave no reason. He said "In light of the events," which I took to mean that since my boss was fired, I was fired.

I asked what he was firing me for. He said, "I just don't think it's going to work out." I was upset, although, frankly, I would not have stayed much longer under the circumstances. There was a conflict. The editor-in-chief and I were on one side; the president on the other.

When I told the president that I thought this was unfair, he threatened to question my ability. This was a kind of coercion. I wasn't ready to fight. It was like, take the money and run.

First, Try to Save the Worker

Those terminations were brutal, without warning, needlessly destructive. A more humane way to deal with employees is to plan ahead, attempting to salvage workers who are not as productive as they could be.

Long before dismissal becomes inevitable, a supervisor should try to rehabilitate an employee who is working below capacity. Differences can be worked out. Employees can improve their working skills or job attitudes. Many employees can be saved.

An example is described in Alvin Toffler's book, *The Third Wave:*

> One black mother working for a Boston bank was on the verge of being fired because—although a good worker in other respects—she was continually turning up late. Her poor attendance record reinforced racist stereotypes about the unreliability and laziness of Black workers. But when her office went on flextime she was no longer considered late. It turned out . . . that she'd been late because she had to drop her son at a day-care center and could just never get to the office by starting time.

In that case, the solution involved a policy decision by the bank to convert to flextime. Once the problem was identified and discussed with the employee, an arrangement could be made to solve the problem. To save a good worker, most employers will bend the rules a bit.

Employers establish review procedures to identify such situations and to encourage frank discussions. A supervisor should find out what is bothering a worker who is not performing. An employee can discuss personal problems. It makes sense for the employer to try to understand the employee's problem.

Here are some practical guidelines for an effective employee review procedure:

1. *Prompt handling.* When a supervisor seems to be avoiding a frank discussion with an employee, unnecessary anxieties can be created. Management should welcome the chance to talk about problems. Supervisors should be encouraged to initiate such discussions, not to wait until they have time to investigate all the facts. Get the facts. Double check them. Do it quickly. Workers don't like to be kept on hold. An employee may decide to go to a lawyer or an outside agency if a prompt response is not forthcoming from the boss.

2. *Accessibility.* A common problem with internal grievance procedures is how to persuade workers to use them. The contact person should be easily available. Supervisors should encourage complaints and should be held accountable for seeing that employees make use of the system. When a worker is fired suddenly for something that has been a chronic problem, the supervisor is at fault.

3. *Informality.* Discussions with an employee should be handled in an informal non-threatening atmosphere. Verbal is better than written. The grievance system should be simple. Nobody likes to tell their story over and over again. No one should receive a printed form letter in response to a personal problem. When such a form is perceived as "legal," it may motivate an employee to seek outside help, perhaps a lawyer.

4. *Consistency.* The supervisor should check with the personnel department to be sure that the company position is correct and consistent with past practice. All too frequently, an employee discovers that other workers are being treated

differently or learns that there is a difference of opinion among various representatives of management. An executive should never suggest that some other manager made a mistake. Passing the buck is bad psychology. The worker does not care who is at fault, only what can be done about the problem.

5. *Corrective.* When management was wrong, corrective action should be taken promptly to resolve the problem. The grievance procedure should have a payoff for the employee. It only can justify itself if it works. Then, it will be regarded as a respectable part of the organization.

6. *Finality.* The management group should give the employee a final decision, with a full explanation, as soon as the facts are known.

7. *Educational.* The process should result in change within the organization. Managers ought to ask: Was the claim justified? Why did this employee misunderstand the situation? Why did the employee feel aggrieved? What can we do to avoid these problems in the future?

Management should discuss each case after it is processed. By resolving internal conflict, an organization can learn how to improve. Be sure that the conditions that caused the problem have been resolved.

Most employee problems should be solved at the work place. Directly. Face to face. The employee and the supervisor should discuss their differences. Misperceptions can be resolved. The employee's abilities and the requirements of the job can be matched. In some cases, a well-intentioned but unproductive worker can be transferred to a more appropriate position.

The Open-Door Policy

Many firms have adopted what they call an "open-door" policy, under which the chief executive is available to hear employee complaints, investigate them, and see that justice is done. Some workers view the open door as an exercise in managerial hypocrisy. We live in a suspicious era. Any system where management makes the final decision may be suspect. Employees may not believe that top management can be independent and impartial.

If you are a top executive who sits at the "pay-off" position under an open-door policy, you should try to lend credibility to the system. It is not enough to be warm and understanding, to exercise sophisticated listening skills. You have an obligation to investigate the facts, to get to the heart of things. If the supervisor was wrong, you should be prepared to overrule the termination.

If you are a busy manager, you may not have time to gather evidence carefully and comprehensively. You will be tempted to tell the personnel department to call in the supervisor, ask a few questions, and rubber-stamp the decision.

Would you operate that way if you were an outside investigator? Of course not. The employee is claiming that the supervisor made a bum decision. You are obligated to investigate the circumstances with an objective point of view. Otherwise, you and your open-door policy are a fraud. Is your only purpose to whitewash management decisions? Can an individual employee obtain an impartial review by coming through your open door? The answers depend upon how you handle your responsibilities.

Above all, don't punish an employee who uses the open door. Word will get around. If the open door is phony, the corporation should never have established the system.

Why Is There So Much Guilt in Firing?

Feelings play an important part in the working environment. People at work don't leave their emotions at home. When an employee is being fired, those relationships come to the surface.

A classic type is the boss who hires a new worker with expectations so high as to be completely unrealistic, anticipating a level of performance that the employee will be unable to meet. When the employee demonstrates a lack of perfection, that kind of boss decides that the worker can do nothing right, or the boss may shift from one favorite to another. This tendency smacks of the immature romantic who falls in love with an image of perfection, then rejects and is repulsed by normal behavior. The scenario may be even more likely when people of the opposite sex are involved.

A man hires a new secretary. She is wonderful. Several weeks later, she is terrible. Why? She is the same person. The employer may have made promises during the honeymoon episode. The boss may recall some of those indiscretions, understanding why the worker seems disappointed. Now the boss regrets the whole thing and feels guilty.

Another aspect of working life may contribute to the boss's guilt. Many tasks are carried out as a team. One person's failure may reflect the weaknesses of others. If a worker fails to do the job, it may be the supervisor's fault. More guilt is generated.

In a factory, a supervisor may have failed to train a worker or to help with the set-up or to make sure that the machinery was in order. In an advertising agency or executive office, where the standards of performance may be less measurable, the manager may have failed to establish effective policies or productive relationships. If an employee fails, it may be because the manager was unable to create an appropriate working environment. By firing the employee, the manager may be attempting to relieve himself of the blame.

Executives are responsible for their people. They share the blame for any failures. This may explain why managers feel guilty when firing an employee. They wonder how far the blame will spread. Should I be firing him? Should management be firing both of us? Is it my fault?

Terminating someone is an unpleasant part of an executive's job. Even the thought of it creates stress. It is one of the major sources of anxiety for chief executives. I can testify to that. Nevertheless, it is part of your job. You should accomplish it just as efficiently as you would handle any other important business transaction.

Not every manager dislikes firing people. There are the crazies; the abusive, domineering, bullies who like to destroy peoples' egos. Some bosses are neurotic, malicious, or sadistic, quite willing to crucify their subordinates. At a management training program, one executive, after several drinks, told me that he liked to fire people: "I must be unusual. Other people in the company hate it. They know I don't mind. They give me the tough ones. I've never said this before, but when I fire someone, I feel good. It's almost like sex, a chance to dominate another person. I mean, totally. Afterwards, I am on a high, but feeling guilty too. Saying it, it sounds kind of sick."

In a company where terminations are not reviewable, injustice seems certain. In some organizations, people can be fired at the discretion of their supervisor. Should anyone be trusted with that much arbitrary power? I don't think so.

Managers usually handle the terminations of any employees that report to them. They may be tempted to let someone else handle that chore. An office manager may be asked to fire an executive's secretary. That is a cop-out. Most executives believe that terminating their own people is part of their job. Employees expect it. A secretary who was fired by an office manager blurted out: "Why didn't the bastard have the guts to tell me himself? I don't mind losing my job but I have no respect for someone who can't do his own dirty work."

Employees Should Be Told
Why They Are Being Fired

A person being discharged should be given an opportunity to discuss the reasons. In general, executives who are terminating an employee should be straightforward and honest about why the action is being taken. It takes guts, but do it!

When an employee is terminated for poor performance, it should not come as a surprise. Too frequently, it does. A supervisor may have given satisfactory performance ratings to justify an employee's normal salary increase. When the supervisor decides that the employee must be terminated, the earlier ratings need to be explained away. If a worker is not meeting the standards of company performance, a supervisor should not wait until the final termination interview to discuss the problem. By being candid, the employer gives the worker an opportunity to improve. An employee who has been warned will not be surprised when terminated.

Too often, a discharged worker will say, "I don't know why they did it. Last month, during the performance review, my boss told me I was doing fine. Today, he let me go. How can that be? All my boss would say was 'It's out of my hands.' What a system!"

When the day finally arrives when an employee must be terminated, most experts think that the interview should take place promptly and that the employee should be asked to leave. The latter may not be appropriate in every case. A long-term employee with a good record can be given more time, kept on for a while. But there are dangers.

In *How to Survive Getting Fired—And Win,* Jerry Cowle suggests a "sorched earth" policy, advising an individual being fired to go through the files, extracting any undeveloped ideas that might be useful on the next job. "Simply have the maintenance people bring up a couple of cardboard cartons, fill them with your personal files, and take the cartons home." Since you might not want to permit such access to company files, you should protect your lists of customers, proprietary information or any personnel records that might fuel a possible law suit. Do it diplomatically; but do it.

Usually, the sooner the employee leaves the premises the better. Such a policy can protect the employer. In one case, a woman who was terminated from an executive position in a major corporation was encouraged to interview for a similar position elsewhere in the company. Operating from a temporary office, she spent her time sending memos to top executives, seeking an opportunity to discuss her problem. Inevitably, she became an irritant, particularly since management was in the throes of a vicious power struggle. Finally, having branded herself as a trouble maker; she was asked to leave. Bitter and discouraged, she tried to find a similar position in another company. She found that her reputation was soiled throughout the industry.

> They encouraged me to think that another job would be offered to me. They wanted women, they said. I was qualified, they said. The top people were telling me that they would help. Others wouldn't even talk with me. I should have left right away. Then, I could have found another job.

Who Should Represent the Employer?

If a manager is not qualified to negotiate a termination, someone else should make the deal. The employer should be represented by an executive who can be friendly but not weak toward the person being discharged. If the supervisor can't handle it, another manager should step in.

When a top executive is being eased out of a major corporation, the final bargaining may be turned over to lawyers who shuttle between the principals as they would in any other corporate negotiation. They act as professional negotiators.

According to a recent article in the *Wall Street Journal,* dismissal of top-level officers has become common in recent years. Supposedly, the increase in firings results from boards of directors taking a closer interest in running the company. According to Max Ulrich of Ward Howell Associates, the executive recruiting firm, most executives earning over $100,000 a year demand termination protection in their contracts. The employer may have to pay a year or more salary if the executive is asked to leave.

For example, Thomas H. Wyman, who became chief executive of CBS in June, 1980, following in-and-out experiences by earlier CBS presidents John D. Backe and Arthur R Taylor, obtained a million dollars to take the job, a high salary and a commitment that if he is terminated "without cause," the company will pay him three times his base pay.

When termination negotiations involve large sums of money, discussions are carried out in a businesslike way. Both parties should be pragmatic. Life will not end for the person being discharged. The employer's business will continue. The attitudes of former executives toward the firm can be important, particularly if the executive stays in the same field.

A Touch of Humanity

An executive who must arrange a termination should be sensitive to the personal problems of the employee. A law-school dean told me how he saved the career of a member of his faculty. The man had given up a successful career as a practicing lawyer to teach, but received low ratings from student reviewers who felt that he was unprepared. It was his first experience as a teacher. He seemed to be improving but had acquired a poor reputation. The other professors did not respect him. After many conversations, the dean convinced the man that he had no future at that law school. He persuaded him to resign at the end of the year, agreeing to help him get another appointment. Good advice. The professor gained tenure at another university.

In some areas of employment, employees are given time to find new positions. For example, associates in law firms who are passed over for partnership are expected to find a place elsewhere. The firm will help them. Generally, they are given ample time to make a connection. Because law firms may have to deal with former associates in future matters, they are sensitive to the personal problems of associates who must be passed over.

Whoever represents the employer should know the benefit program. The company should get credit for each item. Preventive-claims management involves psychology as well as law, particularly in understanding the claimant's perceptions. The employer wants the employee to accept the termination. Employees like to be listened to, to be treated with dignity. Their willingness to accept management's offer may depend as much upon how they are treated as whether they obtained a generous settlement.

The employer should remember that company gossip may get back to a discharged employee. Malicious gossip can trigger a lawsuit. In one case, an executive vice president who had fired a feisty female salesperson, bragged that he had "canned her for being such a pain in the ass."

In another situation, an executive reported at a staff meeting that her department had gotten rid of an "old fuddy-duddy" who was holding up a program to computerize record keeping. She explained that she was trying to open up opportunities for younger people. In both cases, the indiscretions became part of the testimony in lawsuits filed by the angry former employees.

The feelings and perceptions of the line supervisor should also be considered. Settlement discussions can effect the supervisor's morale. Will he feel vindicated? Or will he conclude that the company blamed him for the problem? If so, he may be the next person to get fired.

The Option of Early Retirement

Sometimes it is possible to arrange a termination so that it seems entirely voluntary. Early retirement may provide a humane, cost-effective method for terminating an employee.

According to Johnson & Higgins, a major insurance broker

and pension consultant, two-thirds of the eligible employees in a recent corporate survey retired before normal retirement age. Not every early retirement is voluntary. Some older employees are forced into retirement. It is expensive for an individual to sue a corporation for wrongful discharge, even under the Age Discrimination in Employment Act. The employee may prefer to negotiate a satisfactory termination.

Both parties should go into negotiations with a clear understanding of their legal rights and with negotiating strategy. The employer should remember that other senior employees will know what kind of deal is being offered. The employee should calculate how much money the company will save.

Sometimes, there is no easy way out. An employee will not agree to early retirement, will refuse to resign, and will reject any negotiated settlement. The line supervisor may have to recommend that such a person be terminated.

How an Executive Should Review a Termination

Permission to discharge a employee may have to be obtained from higher levels of management. As an executive, you may be asked to approve the decision. It will be tempting to simply confirm the supervisor's judgment, in the absence of some obvious violation of the firm's personnel procedures. A responsible manager should investigate further. By providing an independent review, you may protect the company from future liability.

Can the termination be justified? It may be difficult to evaluate the situation. Your facts will be second- or third-hand. Ordinarily, management gets its information from the supervisor. Questions of credibility may be involved. How can you make a fair judgment based on hearsay?

The facts may be uncertain. The employee says that termination is not justified. You should listen to the employee's side of the story. Who is telling the truth? The truth is not written on your office wall. The supervisor may be lying, sometimes for obvious reasons. The facts must be established on the basis of various assumptions. Should the supervisor's version of the facts be accepted by the company without independent proof?

If your employees were represented by a union, a shop steward would have investigated the facts from the employee's point of view. Several grievance conferences would have been held between the union and the company. If not settled, the grievance would have been set down for a hearing before an impartial arbitrator to determine whether there was just cause for discharge.

In order to make such a decision, a labor arbitrator would listen to the testimony of witnesses and the arguments presented by both sides. The evidence would have been weighed against the past practice of the parties, the prevailing norms in the industry and specific disciplinary standards.

Let's suppose that an employee has been discharged for poor job performance. The standard of proof must satisfy the arbitrator. Not so easy! How does a company prove that the worker was treated fairly?

An employee in an insurance association in Texas was fired for being inefficient, having poor work habits, and generally disrupting the office. He was obviously a disruptive employee. Even the grievant admitted that at one meeting he "became angry and agressively escalated our conflict by shaking my fist . . . ."

Even so, the company had to prove its case. There were negative evaluations in the employee's file. Some of the evidence against him consisted of letters from co-workers to the union, complaining that the grievant was rude to policyholders on the telephone and was inefficient, that he acted in irrational ways, yelling in the hallways, slamming doors, and throwing things.

At the hearing, the grievant maintained that his supervisors and his fellow employees were wrong. He said that he was always right and that everyone else was picking on him and disliked him for no good reason. After carefully reviewing the record, the arbitrator upheld the discharge.

An executive can't be as meticulous as an arbitrator, and may find it difficult to get close to the truth. But an executive should make an effort to be fair. An investigation that pretends to gather the facts without giving the grievant a chance to testify or without testing management's evidence by direct confrontation provides little protection for an employee who has been unfairly discharged.

Some companies provide an outside arbitrator or mediator for their employees. For example, the fifth step in the grievance procedure in the American Optical Company's employee guide is to complain to an impartial arbitrator who is given the right to make a complete investigation of the case. "His or her decision will be final and binding on both you and the company."

An Informal Way to Settle Employee Disputes

An employer may prefer to have employee grievances decided by a third party. It is difficult enough to run a productive business without being hassled by squabbles between employees and supervisors. It may save time to turn some problems over to an arbitrator. For example, a woman who believes that she has been discriminated against because of her sex has no easy way to obtain an impartial review of her complaint. Such cases are common. They frequently involve subjective decisions as to job performance, allegations of sexual harassment, or contested terminations. Sometimes, these kinds of disputes can be resolved amicably. Other cases require a careful analysis of the facts and an understanding of the perceptions of the worker and of the supervisor.

To handle discrimination cases, where the requirements of the law must be observed, many employers, because of the risk of class actions, are providing internal grievance procedures.

When a controversy arises, neither the worker nor the employer relish the idea of having to go before a government agency. The emphasis before such agencies had been upon making sure that no systematic discrimination is taking place. Agencies cannot devote much time or attention to an individual claim. Any real relief has to be obtained in court. For most people, a law suit is the last thing they want. With a backlog of such cases, courts find it difficult to provide prompt justice for large numbers of individual claims.

Most major corporations have internalized the resolution of employment claims. Realizing that such complaints originate at the workplace, managers try to identify problems promptly, making it possible for employees to discuss their concerns with management. If the supervisor's action was not appropriate, some adjustment may be possible. Most potential discrimination claims are resolved through informal discussions.

The life cycle of complaints, where a worker has been treated unfairly, often starts with a feeling of personal rejection. Only afterward does the complaint become couched in terms of legal rights. If the employer does not respond to the personal concern, the employee may consult a lawyer. From then on, the likelihood of an amicable settlement lessens. The feeling of personal injustice becomes converted into a legal claim, often involving the violation of a federal statute.

Some employers offer to mediate or arbitrate whatever issues cannot be settled. An informal arbitration system can be obtained by referring to the American Arbitration Association's rules. For more than half a century, the American Arbitration Association has provided arbitration services for many kinds of cases. Arbitration has been particularly useful for resolving grievances between unions and employers.

Employment dispute arbitration is the same remedy in a new package. Personal disagreements between workers and supervisors start small, but they can escalate into important issues. They need to be handled quickly. Sometimes the worker and the supervisor are adamant about the differences between them. This can be particularly true in a large organization, such as an insurance company or bank. The personnel department may not want to overrule a position taken by the supervisor. Then, a system of informal, impartial review can be helpful.

A plan for arbitrating nonunion problems was recently installed for approximately five hundred employees by Life Savers, Inc., in Port Chester, New York. Under this plan, employees may submit grievances under expedited arbitration rules of the American Arbitration Association, thereby obtaining a fair and impartial review of their complaint. The system is quite simple. First, an employee complains to the immediate supervisor. The supervisor must respond within two working days. If the answer is not satisfactory, the employee may complain in writing. The supervisor must answer in writing within two days. If the supervisor's answer does not settle the affair, the employee may file the complaint with the personnel manager. After consultation with the department head, personnel must provide the employee with the final management position in writing within three days.

At this point, an employee can appeal directly to the plant manager or may submit the case to impartial arbitration. A request for arbitration must be filed within two weeks and must be in writing, delivered to the personnel office. The hearing is held before an impartial arbitrator appointed by the American Arbitration Association. Hearings take place at the plant. Employees do not lose pay for participating in an arbitration hearing. No recordings or transcripts are made. The arbitrator must hand down a decision within five working days. The award may be posted on the bulletin board.

Arbitration allows the personnel department to detach itself from the dispute. The people who caused the problem are expected to resolve it, with the help of an impartial expert. It is important to select arbitrators who can be impartial between the individual worker and the employer. Where do you find such people? The American Arbitration Association is a primary source for arbitrators who are familiar with arbitration, know how to listen carefully to testimony and understand the employment relationship.

For the worker, such a system provides an opportunity to submit a complaint to an impartial expert for a decision. The matter can be determined promptly, without the acrimony that litigation often generates among employees. The employer can resolve potentially embarrassing situations by obtaining a prompt interpretation of its personnel procedures or of its obligations under the affirmative action program. Since the case is discussed in the privacy of a conference room, the therapeutic effect can be immense. Settlement is always possible, which can be beneficial to both sides.

The decision of an arbitrator is enforceable when both parties have agreed to abide by it and have participated in the process. Where the dispute involves an employee's rights under a federal statute, a further hearing before a government agency or in court may be possible. Even then, the arbitrator's award would be accepted as strong evidence.

The question of legal enforcement may not be critical. Most employees will abide by the results if management is willing to have an arbitrator decide whether the supervisor's decision was consistent with the firm's policies.

American workers expect fair treatment. A recent report from the University of Michigan's Survey Research Center under a Labor Department grant indicates a growing willingness among workers to challenge the decisions of supervisors. Many executives champion voluntary solutions. Worker grievance systems can be strengthened by adding arbitration to the employer's present internal grievance procedures. This can be done voluntarily, under the present law.

In higher education, impartial arbitration already has been utilized as the last step in faculty grievance procedures. The Northeastern University Faculty Grievance Procedure is a case in point. The final review is arbitration before an AAA arbitrator. Arbitration systems are also found in hospitals, religious organizations, and other service agencies.

Increasing numbers of corporations have established internal mediation systems to help resolve discrimination claims. When a complaint has not been settled in the mediation process, employers can offer to submit the case to arbitration. That may be good for morale, because employees will recognize that the firm is willing to accept an impartial decision.

I asked an experienced labor arbitrator whether he had difficulty deciding cases under nonunion systems. "Of course not," he said, "the issues are much the same. Instead of interpreting a collective bargaining contract, I look at the employer's personnel policies. If an employee is not an expert in presenting the facts, that is no different than where shop stewards present grievances for small unions."

Would he put a nonunion employee back to work if the company couldn't show just cause? "That would depend on my authority. An employee might have a tough time when he goes back on the job. I try to anticipate what would happen. In some cases, I might decide that it would be better to award severance pay. Parties seem to have faith in my ability to select an appropriate remedy."

3

Why Are Employees Discharged?

UNDER AMERICAN COMMON LAW, most employers are not required to justify their reasons for terminating a worker. Nevertheless, management usually attempts to make a showing, at least to its own satisfaction. As John Whittlesey, the chief labor counsel of Union Carbide, recently explained to an audience of lawyers at the Association of the Bar of the City of New York: "Employers don't fire people just for the hell of it." He is right. Employers don't, but sometimes a supervisor will.

A foreman may take a dislike to a particular worker and pick on him, finding fault, making a paper record of minor deficiencies, harassing him so that he will quit. He may fire the worker. It happens all the time. If an employee is a member of a union, the employer must prove that the discharge was for just cause. Even where there is no union, a supervisor may have to obtain prior approval for a termination. Higher levels of management usually require some good reason for firing a worker.

The most common justification for people being terminated is lack of work. When that can be demonstrated, an employee can be laid off. Sometimes questions arise about which employee should be terminated. Should the layoff be based upon seniority or comparative ability? How deep to cut? But the principle is well established: where the need for workers has evaporated, it is understood that the employer has the right to reduce the work force. Although we do not say that such a worker was "fired," the effect on the worker may be the same thing.

The cases that will be described in this chapter involve situations where employees are terminated for cause. Management decided to pronounce the death sentence.

Disciplinary Discharge

Workers are often fired because they have violated the company's disciplinary rules. They are being terminated for cause. There are two kinds of infractions that call for discipline. Certain violations can be corrected. An employee may be disciplined for absence from work, tardiness, poor performance, violation of safety rules, inattention to duties, loafing on the job, disobedience, or creating a disturbance on company property. An employer ordinarily would not fire a worker for the first such infraction. These kinds of problems are dealt with by progressive discipline. The first such incident may result in a warning or a minor disciplinary penalty. If repeated, more severe discipline may be imposed.

A second category of violations is described as gross misconduct. These might include fighting, willful destruction of company property, theft or dishonest acts, disorderly or immoral conduct on company property or "any other action equally culpable." For one such infraction, a company might fire an employee. Sometimes an employee will be suspended from duty until an investigation can be made. If the facts are established, a single act of gross misconduct may result in discharge.

Management must have the power to discipline employees or to discharge them. This right is expressed in the management rights clause in collective bargaining agreements and sometimes in the booklets that describe the employment relationship in non-union shops. Most executives think that the power to discipline workers is crucial. Without that right, they believe that it would be impossible to run a business.

No company can forecast every kind of employee misconduct. Most employee booklets retreat into generalities which must be defined when cases arise. Management likes to interpret its own rules. We are talking about power. Management wants to decide what the rules mean, how workers must comply, applying the rules to cases as they may arise.

An employer needs to provide an orderly and efficient workplace. It would be nice if employees could work under a system of self-restraint. But human nature being what it is, rules are necessary. If rules are to be acceptable, they must be based upon reasonable standards of objectivity and fair play. On their face, at least, they must meet the employees' notion of what would be fair and reasonable. The workers understand why such rules must exist and expect the employer to provide them.

Job applicants ask whether a corporation is a "good place to work." They inquire about wages and fringe benefits. They also ask about the atmosphere of the place. Are the supervisors fair? Can a person work there without worrying about petty regulations that insult a person's integrity? Work rules must be appropriate for the kind of work being done, and for the employees themselves. To enforce the rules, some form of discipline is necessary. Violators must be punished.

The right to fire a worker is the most potent penalty in the management arsenal. As the ultimate weapon, it is seldom used. Most problems are handled in softer ways. The employer has an investment in the individual. The trained employee has become a business asset. As John Whittlesey says, "Employers don't fire people just for the hell of it." But sometimes, an employer will come to the conclusion that a worker must be fired. An employee who becomes a chronic violator of the work rules may have to be terminated.

Progressive Discipline

Discipline involves fixing appropriate penalties for improper actions by employees. Penalties may include oral or written warnings, suspensions, or probation, depending on the nature of the offense and the policies of the employer. Small employers can handle cases as they come along, deciding what is appropriate. Larger companies must be more methodical.

Progressive discipline is a system of penalties imposed with increasing severity. In theory, employees learn not to violate the rules. If the initial offense is not repeated, the heavier penalty can be avoided. When infractions are repeated, the final penalty may be discharge.

A policy of progressive discipline must be administered fairly. This does not mean that every employee gets exactly the same penalty for the same offense. There may be extenuating circumstances. It does mean that workers must be judged by consistent standards. Rules should be applied evenly, but with discretion. Discipline should be imposed without favoritism. When workers are penalized differently for the same action, employees become confused. What can they expect next time?

Management can use the threat of discharge to motivate improved performance. Discharge is the maximum punishment for improper conduct. Using it as an example may deter other employees, encouraging them to behave properly. Lesser penalties are used to help employees learn from their mistakes. Employers usually give workers at least one warning before discharging them. Unions require such a practice, at least for relatively minor infractions. For serious offenses, such as dishonesty, unprovoked assault, or intentional damage to company property, no warning may be required.

Some collective bargaining contracts and personnel manuals contain a schedule of penalties which may be rigidly enforced. This may create problems. Fixing the required penalty in advance takes away management's discretion to evaluate the particular offense. Supervision may be forced to impose too severe a penalty, perhaps losing a valuable employee.

In one recent AAA arbitration case, the employee had yelled vulgar language at his foreman in the presence of a fellow employee. The contract listed only three instances where the employer could fire a worker. One of these was neglect of duty; so the man was fired for "neglect of duty." The arbitrator decided that the man's vulgarity did not constitute neglect of duty. The other two grounds listed were not applicable, and the arbitrator was not authorized to substitute a lesser penalty. The employee was reinstated with full back pay.

The employee's supervisor usually makes the initial decision to terminate. If the action is taken without prior consultation, it may not coincide with the firm's personnel policies. The supervisor may try to justify it with the personnel department. If the personnel director is unable to reverse the action, top management may have to deal with a situation where an employee has been terminated for inadequate reasons.

President Derek Bok of Harvard University described the problem in one of his recent reports:

> There is much dissatisfaction with the ways in which these problems are being handled in most corporations. This is hardly surprising. Personnel officers have traditionally ranked near the bottom of the executive hierarchy. They often regard themselves as responsible advocates for employee interests instead of corporate officials charged with developing workable policies that are consistent with the company's overall goals. As a result, personnel officers typically come in conflict with line managers, forcing issues up to higher levels where general managers feel ill-equipped to resolve them.

Bok believes that management could protect itself by creating internal mechanisms to review employee complaints. This is a relatively new idea for American managers. Where there is no union, management has not had to justify such decisions. With more attention being paid to worker rights, this may change.

Even in nonunion firms, a supervisor does not have complete freedom to fire a worker. The rules are fixed by management. The supervisor's decision must conform to company policies. Certain procedures may be required. Since equal employment laws have come into effect, personnel directors want to make sure that proper guidelines have been followed. The supervisor's actions may be reviewed by management and commented on by the personnel department. Executives will ask why the employee was discharged. Was there just cause? What was the employee's record?

Another consideration is plant "morale." Where someone has been treated unfairly by a supervisor, morale can suffer. The discharge of one employee, where patently unfair, may raise critical issues with other members of the work force. The strike by Polish workers in the summer of 1980 was triggered by a single discharge, that of labor organizer Anna Walentynowicz on August 7, 1980.

Before deciding to discharge a worker, management should analyze the situation. What rules of conduct have been established? Are they in writing? Do employees know about them? Did the employee violate the rules? Did the worker have a good record? Is dismissal the correct penalty? All too frequently, a discharge takes place before such questions are asked. A supervisor fires an employee. Afterward, executives at higher levels in the company are asked to review the decision. Earlier, they would have had the power to substitute their judgment for that of the supervisor. Now, each echelon is likely to support the decision below. In a nonunion company, the first independent review may take place in court, years later.

If the worker had been represented by a union, a shop steward would have challenged the discharge immediately. In the grievance procedure, questions would have been raised. At various meetings, the facts would have been discussed and discussed again. Some compromise might have been worked out. Under American labor law, a union is required to represent every member of the bargaining unit, forcing the company to prove its case.

Collective bargaining creates important rights for employees. The employer agrees to abide by the contract that it has signed. But the benefits of the agreement would be meaningless if the contract did not restrict the employer's right to discharge members of the union.

Arbitration decisions illustrate the continuing conflict between management and the union. The employer retains the right to manage the enterprise and to direct the work force. It can issue whatever rules are necessary to regulate the employees' behavior. But the employer must be able to justify any action that it takes against the job interests of an individual worker. It must show just cause.

Employers insist upon their management rights. Since it is responsible for operating the firm, management must establish rules, and can discipline or discharge employees who fail to meet them. Otherwise, management would have no way to meet its obligations to the owners and stockholders, or to the other employees who are investing their lives in the business.

Work Rules

Work rules are important because both workers and supervisors rely on them, but their application must be related to the business needs of the employer. A rule that employees wear hard hats while working in the factory seems reasonable. But if an employer disciplines a worker for not wearing his helmet while taking a shower, the application of the rule would be inappropriate.

Another example: Some firms prefer that employees speak English. Can an employer require workers to speak only English? A lumber yard in Brownsville, Texas, where 75 percent of the population were Mexican-American established a rule that employees must speak English at all times. A worker who violated the rule was fired. The Equal Employment Opportunity Commission thought that the rule discriminated against Hispanic employees and filed a lawsuit to prove the point. The grievant was a native-born American of Mexican descent named Hector García, who worked as a salesman. He was fired after a few months on the job. The company claimed that he had failed to keep control of inventory, to replenish the stock on display, or to keep his area clean. In addition, he had violated the rule that English be spoken on the job.

Mr. García said that he had been fired because he talked to one of his co-workers in Spanish. In Federal court, the EEOC tried to show that the company's rule was a discriminatory condition of employment. Various Hispanic civil rights organizations entered the case. Some five years after the dispute arose, the United States Court of Appeals confirmed that Mr. García was properly discharged. "An employer's rule forbidding a bilingual employee to speak anything but English in public areas while on the job is not discrimination based on national origin as applied to a person who is fully capable of speaking English and chooses not to do so in deliberate disregard of his employer's rule."

Reasonable work rules, coupled with progressive discipline, are fundamental to sound labor relations. Rules are generally published in employee booklets or posted on bulletin boards. They must be communicated to the workers. Arbitrators have upheld grievances where an employer could not show that the rules were posted or given to the workers in a printed form. Not every rule must be in writing. Some are self-evident, such as the rule that an employee should not assault a co-worker.

In developing work rules, employers sometimes assume that they have an unrestricted right to regulate their employees. Not true. The law places various limitations upon the employer. When an employer has a contract with a union, management's authority may be circumscribed further because the employer bargained away some of its rights. Restrictions may appear in the union contract.

Management Rights

In collective bargaining contracts, the power to impose discipline flows from the management rights clause. A typical clause might state that "the management of the work, the direction of the working force and the right to hire and discharge are vested exclusively in the employer." This language purports to give management full discretion to make decisions about discipline or discharge. Even so, arbitrators may require a reasonable standard of behavior. "Just cause" will be implied even if it is not specified. In most contracts, the employer will have agreed to discharge only for "cause," "just cause," "proper cause," or some similar standard. Sometimes, contracts contain a list of the permissable grounds for discharge coupled with a progressive discipline policy.

Progressive discipline is also used by nonunion companies. Its effectiveness depends upon the employees' faith in its fairness. Inconsistency is demoralizing. The workers soon discover that the employer is playing favorites. Progressive discipline works because employees realize that each successive violation will lead to an increasing penalty. The employer must be sure that the penalties are properly imposed. If a one-day suspension is followed by a warning, the purpose of the plan is destroyed. Progressive discipline systems can be flexible, but not illogical. For the system to work, the various steps must be followed. This is particularly true during the critical final steps. When a discharge is called for, the stage should be carefully set. The employee should be warned that the next offense will result in termination. The system should provide clear signals to the employee that trouble lies ahead.

An overly rigid discipline policy can become an administrative nightmare, so complicated that the personnel department is constantly defending grievances. When plant rules have proliferated, supervisors may become bogged down in a tedious campaign to enforce trivial behavioral lapses. Morale tends to suffer during periods when management is attempting to tighten up on slack discipline. Shop stewards become popular with the workers. Each time a supervisor pronounces a new penalty, the steward files a grievance, demonstrating once again the benefits of having a union. The workers feel harassed. The employer is viewed as the enemy. Supervisors dislike having to police such a code. Plants with this kind of atmosphere generate hundreds of grievances, poisoning the working relationship.

When the same situation arises in a nonunion plant, the individual worker begins to feel like a clay duck in a shooting gallery. When will his turn come to be picked off by a zealous rule keeper? There is no better way to encourage employees to join a union than to subject them to the frustrations of overly rigid behavioral rules, combined with a harsh discipline policy. Employers become enforcement machines. Individual dignity goes down the drain. The situation gets worse when rules are applied capriciously. When progressive discipline loses its credibility, the system fails. Each time a decision must be overturned by the personnel department, any reputation that supervisor may have for evenhanded discipline is torpedoed.

Personnel directors berate managers: "Why didn't you talk to me first? You can't do it that way! We have to justify these things." A personnel director hesitates to overrule a supervisor. But company policy requires that the progressive discipline system be administered in accordance with its terms. When the supervisor is reversed, the employees wonder how management could be so stupid. "This plant is being run by idiots," one shop steward told me. "My union used to have a problem getting members to come to meetings. Now, thanks to those boneheads, some member gets shafted every week. We tell the worker that only the union can save him. He and his buddies turn out for our monthly meetings, so that he can play the star role in a discussion of his case. Thank God for dumb foremen."

Sometimes the grievance process, with all its bickering and confrontation and excitement, takes on a life of its own. Employees who become bored standing in front of their machines become engrossed in the dramatic, ideological conflict between the shop steward and the foreman about whether Ms. Gomez was abusing her coffee breaks, or whether an employer can require sweepers to wear safety shoes. A grievance system can become folk theater. Disputes over firings are the most exciting of all: management principles to be defended; a question of justice; a victim; a dreaded punishment; the forces of labor massed against the elite management corps. A day at the plant offers no more dramatic event than a juicy discharge grievance.

In a nonunion company, the process is less exciting. Management tends to support supervisors. Controversy goes underground. That does not mean that the workers are happy and content. Sometimes, an employer can be brutal.

A new cashier was hired by a nonunion restaurant in Arkansas. In order to get the job, she had to agree in writing that she could be discharged at any time without notice. Later, when the manager of the restaurant discovered that $99 was missing from the cash register, the cashier was accused of stealing the money and discharged. She denied the charge. When she asked to be paid the seventeen hours she already had worked, the manager told her to take a polygraph test. She passed the test, but the company would not take her back. Later, she was denied unemployment benefits. The company claimed that she was laid off because she violated the work rules and had a bad attitude. She initiated an investigation by the U.S. Department of Labor. Grudgingly, the company paid her $33 it had deducted from her wages. She also filed suit in state court, seeking damages for intentional infliction of emotional distress and for wrongful discharge. The trial court dismissed her complaint. Some years later, the Arkansas Supreme Court decided that she might be entitled to damages for mental distress. The employer had a right to discharge her, but if its conduct afterward were so outrageous that no reasonable person could be expected to endure it, there might be some liability.

It is unlikely that this case would have arisen if the employee had been represented by a union. No union would allow its members to be discharged without a showing of just cause. It would resist the suggestion that employees take polygraph tests and would have taken the case to arbitration.

In a similar case involving a Kresge store in Detroit, a twenty three-year-old bookkeeper was accused of two small thefts. She was required to take a polygraph test administered by an investigator in a motel room in a seedy neighborhood. Nervous and afraid, she flunked the test and resigned. Later, she sued the company and was awarded $100,000 for "intentional infliction of mental anguish." The lession: a company should be careful about how it fires its workers.

Testing a Discharge in Arbitration

A business executive who wants to be fair to employees should keep abreast of labor arbitrators' awards because they provide helpful guidelines. They spell out the common law of employee rights.

Discharge cases decided by arbitrators describe what factors must be considered to justify a discharge. Of course, cases vary.

In a unionized situation, a grievance will be appraised in the light of the bargaining relationship between the parties. Even on similar facts, arbitrators may reach different opinions. The final decision may depend upon what that particular arbitrator thinks is fair. But arbitrators tend to agree on the underlying principles involved in discharge cases. The cases that follow explain some of those basic principles.

Many cases turn on credibility. Who is to be believed? Sometimes the evidence seems farfetched. Early one morning, on the way to check some recording devices at some fresh-water ponds on the property of Tampa Electric Company, an employee who was driving a small truck suddenly went off the road and struck a guard post on a culvert, flipping the truck over on its top. He was injured. When he limped back to the depot, the company fired him.

Here is the story the driver told at the arbitration hearing: As he rolled along, a snake appeared on the seat next to him in the cab. He grabbed it below the head with his right hand, to protect himself. The snake seemed to be wiggling free, so he took his left hand off the wheel in order to hold the snake with both hands. The truck ran off the road. The employee cut his head and injured his neck. The snake was never found. Would you believe that story?

The company described the testimony as "an incredibly contrived and fabricated afterthought." Perhaps. But the arbitrator believed the grivant and gave him back his job. Would a nonunion employee in the same situation have been able to convince a company to take him back? Probably not. The damaged truck and the unlikely explanation would have weighed against him.

Nonunion employees deserve a fair hearing. Where a discharge is being reviewed, an independent judgment is called for. A manager who is asked to review a contested discharge should require a comprehensive investigation so that reliable evidence can be brought to his attention. Nothing less should be acceptable.

The principles developed in labor arbitration and in the courts can serve as precedents for corporate employers who have agreed to listen with an open mind. An internal review should require management to exercise independent judgment, not only about the events which occurred, but also about the appropriateness of discharge. Some executives believe that management should uphold a discharge unless the supervisor was totally wrong. That is not the standard that would be applied by an arbitrator. There may be some reason to discipline the employee. The question is whether there is sufficient cause for the employee to be fired.

Internal Complaint Procedures

A typical procedure may specify that complaints first be discussed with the employee's immediate supervisor. Most problems are resolved at that point. Where a complaint cannot be settled, the employee is usually permitted to talk to the department manager or to the personnel department. By then, the dispute should be put in writing. An attempt to clarify the facts may result in settlement. If not, an employee may be authorized to appeal the departmental decision to a higher level, perhaps to the general manager. Employers are making greater use of such procedures, to ensure that employee complaints are receiving an adequate review.

A recent survey published by the Bureau of National Affairs indicates that:

- Nine out of ten employers have some mechanism for handling the complaints of unorganized employees.
- Most employers use an open-door policy under which top management makes the final decision about employee complaints.

- Nearly one-third of the employers have been sued recently for unfair treatment.
- Nearly one-quarter of the employers say that they are in the process of revising their procedures or have recently done so.

Although these internal complaint procedures were not designed exclusively for terminations, they can be used for that purpose, and often are. This is particularly true of companies that use arbitration.

A comprehensive survey recently published by The Conference Board, concluded that companies that arbitrate nonunion grievances have been satisfied with the process. The arbitration system does not get swamped with cases; the arbitrators' decisions do not invade management prerogatives; and arbitration does not lead to union organizing. This survey answers the expressed fears of personnel directors who have hesitated to use arbitration.

One employee relations manager whose company has used arbitration for nonunion grievances said: "In twenty eight years I've seen no evidence to the effect that arbitration creates a union organizing committee." Many labor relations directors admit that no system of grievance review short of arbitration can be entirely credible.

The Reasons for Discharge

Terminating an employee is a serious decision. If the supervisor's judgment turns out to be wrong, the company may become liable for back pay. An employee who is reinstated may return to work with hostilities in full bloom. Employers should be sure that their reasons for discharging an employee will bear scrutiny.

Why was the employee discharged? For purposes of analysis, the most common reasons for discharge fall into five categories:

1. Defective job performance
2. Violation of plant rules

3. Fighting
4. Challenging supervision
5. Personal behavior

JOB PERFORMANCE

A prime reason for termination is that the employee failed to meet minimum standards of job performance. Whether such failure was based upon incompetence, negligence, or simple loafing, the lack of performance must be related in some objective way to the production process. Some times, it is difficult to determine whether an employee failed to do the job. This would be particularly true for jobs that require creativity or are not easily measured by objective standards. Many executive or supervisory positions are hard to measure. The boss who says "it just isn't working out," may mean that there is no way to test performance.

For many service jobs, work cannot be calculated in terms of the number of work units produced during a period of time. In such functions, job performance may turn on whether the employee exhibits a bad attitude, is disloyal, fails to follow company policies, or treats customers badly. These failures are not easy to prove. An employee who actually abuses customers may be fired. But other failures can only be judged subjectively, making it difficult to demonstrate a lack of performance.

Some management lawyers say that labor arbitrators seldom uphold a discharge for poor job performance. Not true. But they do require proof. Arbitrators expect the employer to show that there was some measurable standard against which to test the worker. That standard must be fairly applied. If it can be demonstrated that the employee failed to meet an established standard, arbitrators will uphold a discharge.

A typical example: a union official was discharged for poor performance and insubordination. In spite of the grievant's claim that he was fired because of his union activities, the arbitrator found that the company had established just cause by following a program of progressive discipline: a three-day suspension, a ten-day suspension, and then the discharge. The grievant had been cited for failure to work, leaving work early, and loafing, as well as for insubordination. The evidence demonstrated that he was not working up to capacity and had been insolent and arrogant. The company was able to produce a record showing that the grievant failed to carry out work assignments. In a nonunion company, the record of nonperformance might have been less comprehensive and thus less persuasive.

In cases where employees have been discharged for negligence, the employer must prove that the worker was familiar with the rules and knew what would result from his failure. In one case, an employee of the Koppers Company failed to cut off the intake on a tank that was being filled. The tank overflowed. In another, an employee of the Ideal Cement Company neglected to reduce the heat in a kiln. The kiln melted. In both cases, the worker's negligence resulted in serious property damage. Neither employee had a good record. In both cases, the discharge was upheld by labor arbitrators.

If the employer claims that equipment was intentionally damaged, it must be prepared to prove intent. In a General Electric case, an arbitrator upheld the discharge of an employee for intentionally breaking a porcelain liner with a hammer. A witness had "an excellent view of what was going on." The grievant's actions could not be mistaken "for tapping excess foam away with a putty knife, or for an accidental dropping of his hammer, or for letting his arm fall to hit an already dented area." Where deliberate action is alleged, the proof must be certain.

Sometimes the employee's failure to perform will be more than mere negligence or poor work. For example, a schoolbus driver in Michigan stopped her bus on some railroad tracks, removed the ignition key, and began to lecture her high school student passengers about their disruptive behavior. There had been a series of complaints about the woman, culminating in the incident on the tracks. The arbitrator concluded that "deliberately standing a bus on railroad tracks is a serious offense. Such an action, for whatever reason, places the lives of all the bus passengers in serious peril." He found that the driver's "Moment of indiscretion seriously imperiled the lives of her passengers . . . and constituted just cause for discharge."

DISHONESTY

An employer has the right to expect employees to be honest. Dishonesty is considered grounds for immediate termination. One arbitration case involved a radiographer who took X-rays of castings that were to be used in a nuclear power plant. He had been with the company for six years but only recently had been trained as an assistant radiographer. When assigned to take pictures of certain nuclear castings, he warned his supervisor that he was inexperienced. He was told to proceed. After photographing both sides of the casting, using a crane to position the work, he discovered that two of his pictures were defective. Rather than bothering to move the castings again, he faked them, subsituting a duplicate picture with only the identification numbers changed. The casting was delivered to the customer, with the X-rays. Nearly two years after the pictures were taken, the customer discovered and reported the error. The company immediately discharged the grievant for falsifying the X-ray. The union filed a grievance. The purpose of the radiograph was to determine whether there were any flaws below the surface that "could result in the casting's leaking, fracturing or exploding with consequent damage to the nuclear facility." An arbitrator upheld the discharge, even though the casting was not defective. As he pointed out, the purpose of the X-ray was to protect the public. "The importance of the work can scarcely be over-emphasized." Most people would agree with the decision. The public interest in nuclear safety would seem to overwhelm any hesitancy to discharge an employee.

Dishonesty may be difficult to prove. The standard of proof may be more rigorous when an employee is being accused of a crime. Moreover, some of the protections that defendants enjoy in the criminal courts may be claimed by the grievant. An employee accused of a crime may demand the right to confront a witness whose testimony is being relied upon by the employer. The union may claim that a higher standard of proof should be applied in such a case.

Arbitrators can be rough on employees who lie to their employers. A housekeeping assistant in a Lutheran Hospital went on a trip to Las Vegas. People claiming to be her parents called in to say that she was too ill to work. The hospital fired her for misrepresenting the reason for her absence from work. According to the arbitrator, "an employer should not have to tolerate deliberate deception." He upheld the discharge.

It may not be easy to prove that an employee is lying. Both courts and arbitrators have held that a refusal by an employee to take a polygraph test does not create an inference against the person. A Braniff flight attendant was caught by the Dallas/Fort Worth Airport Police with fourteen and a half grains of marijuana in her purse. She could not explain how it got there. She was offered a chance to take a polygraph test at company expense, but declined to do so. Her former husband had been dealing in drugs. She had moved out of his house because of his drug activities. Had he stashed some of his inventory in her luggage? The company fired her for possession of illegal drugs. "After a thorough review of all the evidence and much soul searching" the arbitrator was not convinced of her guilt. Her refusal to take the polygraph test could not be used against her. He put her back to work.

In a somewhat similar case, an engineer working for KCBS in San Francisco was fired for bringing marijuana cookies to the station. While he slept, his girlfriend had baked a batch of chocolate cookies to which she added two teaspoons of marijuana. In the morning, after eating one cookie for breakfast, he went to work carrying cookies for his fellow workers. He ate another cookie on the way to work and shared the rest with his friends. By 9:00 A.M., he felt "a little bit giddy. There was a loss of time and a loss of equilibrium." At that point, he began to suspect there might have been something in the cookies. He talked to the people with whom he had shared them, then called his girlfriend. After nibbling on cookies all morning, she was flying high. She told him what she had done. The situation was becoming confused at KCBS, with various cookie eaters reporting that they were either stoned or sick. The grievant was fired. KCBS took the position that he should have known that marijuana was in the cookies. The arbitrator was not convinced. If the grievant did not know that marijuana was present, he should not be disciplined.

Labor arbitrators understand that employers must be able to rely on the loyalty of their workers. When two members of a Boilermakers Local at a Florida ship repair facility set themselves up in business to do decking work and were overheard soliciting subcontracts from the supervisor of another shipyard, they were fired. The company had a "disloyalty rule" that prohibited competition with the company. The company had condoned moonlighting but said that direct competition was different. The arbitrator found that these employees had formed a company in competition with their employer. The employer had just cause to discharge them.

When the discharge is based upon allegations of theft, most arbitrators will require the employer to prove the case beyond a reasonable doubt. Before an employer fires someone for theft, the evidence had better be clear. But an employee may be required to submit to a reasonable investigation.

A department store clerk was stopped by a guard as she went out for lunch. The guard had noticed square bulges under her pant legs. He deduced that she was stealing some merchandise. He took her to an office and asked her to raise her pants leg for an inspection. She refused. The company rules specified that an employee could be discharged for theft and she was. The case went to arbitration. The grievant didn't deny that she had bulges under her pants leg, but testified that that she didn't know why the guard wanted to search them. The arbitrator didn't believe her. He explained that "people do not have square bulges in their legs as a normal condition of existance." The company had the right to search the grievant. It would have been dereliction of duty for the guard not to have done so. The arbitrator upheld the discharge. Stealing and dishonesty are fundamental failures to meet job standards. Most derelictions are less dramatic.

When employees are discharged for failing to meet performance standards, management must demonstrate that progressive discipline was followed. If the work fails to improve, the employer can terminate the employee. Deteriorating work ethics may be part of the problem. The individual's personal life may seem more important than the job. Where supervision has more traditional views, such an attitude can provoke a discharge.

A quality inspector was told to report for an overtime assignment to cover for a sick employee. He was the only inspector available but had already worked nine hours on that day. When he was called at home and told to return to the plant, he refused. His reason: if he failed to attend a meeting of his bowling league, he wouldn't be invited to play on the team during the season. The employer fired him for disobeying a direct order. A shop rule provided that refusal to follow an order was grounds for immediate discharge. According to the labor contract, an employee could refuse overtime if he had a reasonable excuse. The arbitrator decided that the grievant's excuse was not "reasonable," but put him back to work without back pay because of "his important prior commitment."

Labor arbitrators have been criticized for a tendency to find compromise solutions, for doing what this arbitrator did, putting the employee back to work without back pay. In theory, such an approach is intended to satisfy both parties. In practice, no one may be happy. The employer is stuck with the employee. The grievant goes back to work where he is no longer welcome.

If an employer is going to discharge a worker for poor performance, the standards should be clear. One recent case involved the question of whether a machine operator's fingernails were too long. According to the supervisor, they interfered with her work. First, she was asked to cut her nails. Then she received a three-day and a ten-day suspension for refusing to trim them. When she came back to work, she carried nail clippings in a plastic bag. The supervisor decided that her nails were still too long, and fired her.

The arbitrator held for the grievant: the employer did not have a clear standard as to the length of nails. When the grievant asked how much to trim her nails, she was told "make them short enough to perform." Not good enough! An employer must specify a reasonable length if it wants to enforce such a rule. This grievant was able to hang onto her job by her fingernails.

VIOLATION OF PLANT RULES

Employees give up control over their lives during the hours of employment. They become subject to plant rules and to the instructions of supervision. If they fail to carry out their duties, or violate such rules, they run the risk of discipline. Employees understand that management must have the right to direct how the work is to be done, to assign functions and to enforce reasonable regulations. The progressive discipline system is designed to facilitiate such enforcement.

Some cases make one wonder why management wanted to enforce a rule in such a silly way. On March 13, 1980, the *New York Times* reported that ten electricians at a nuclear construction project had been dismissed by the L. K. Comstock Company for refusing to remove American flag decals from their hard hats. The reason? They were accused of defacing company property, a violation of the published work rules. One worker said, "I'm so damned proud of being fired for this that I'd do it again tomorrow." Another proclaimed, "The flag's a symbol of our country. We've been promoting patriotism on the job and thought it would help boost morale . . . . The decals don't damage or deface the hat, interfere with the quality of our work or slow down production." If you were chief executive of that company, how would you regard the judgement of your project manager?

At other times, it is the employee who is silly. Nevertheless, many would sympathize with an employee of Clay Equipment who threw a pie at the company's management consultant. He took this perilous action in the presence of several people at 3:00

o'clock in the afternoon. According to the grievant, he had been out drinking all night, slept late in the day, got a wild idea, found a pie pan, sprayed it full of meringue, drove to the plant, ran down the aisle and threw the pie at the consultant, hitting him in the face. The rules did not specifically forbid pie throwing.

Some mitigating factors: the grievant had a good work record; horseplay and pranks had happened before in the plant; the management consultant had participated in some of them; the grievant had been egged on by the union president. The arbitrator was all heart: he put the grievant back to work, on probation with a warning. He pointed out that there was an "excellent working relationship among the plant personnel, including management at all levels and employees and union officials." Unfortunately, "the young grievant did not understand the distinction between good clean fun among friends on the one hand and the mindless throwing of a pie upon an unknown person. He does now."

It would not be wise to rely upon that case to justify throwing a pie at your boss. In other companies, assaulting a representative of management with a pie might be taken as an act of violence. People have been fired for "mooning," for scribbling graffiti on the walls of the restrooms, and for eating the plant manager's lunch. Why not pie throwing?

ABSENTEEISM

Absenteeism is a chronic problem for employers. It has been estimated that American industry loses over $200 billion a year because of it. Underlying causes run the gamut from industrial injury to simple laziness. Some absences make little difference in the daily functioning of the business. In other situations, the physical presence of the employee may be vital to the production process and the ripple effects may be substantial.

An employee who is absent from work without excuse, one who leaves the workplace without permission, or one who is caught sleeping on the job may be subject to discipline. For such infractions or for being late to work, an employee will receive progressive discipline. If the practice continues, discharge may be the final punishment.

Rhoda Rosenthal, an attorney with W. R. Grace, recently studied discharge awards for absenteeism. Even where the rules are reasonable and have been communicated to the employees, the employer has the burden of showing that it has applied progressive discipline in a consistent way and has given an unequivocal warning to the grievant. Rosenthal concluded that arbitrators have been supporting management more in recent years. Nevertheless, in only 38 percent of the cases in her 1978 sample did the arbitrator uphold the discharge. Rosenthal thinks that absenteeism should be analogous to stealing, where arbitrators routinely sustain a discharge for making off with insignificant amounts of the employer's property.

Chronic lateness raises unique problems. Much depends upon past practice in the place of employment. In offices where enforcement may be lax, employees get into the habit of coming in late, take unexplained absences during the day, or leave early. Where there is no time clock, an employer may find it difficult to monitor their behavior. It may be difficult to discipline or to discharge a worker for being absent or late unless it can be shown that other employees with the same bad habits are being treated in the same way.

"Don't pick on me, Mrs. Worthington, you should come down here at quarter to five. I am usually the only one who hangs around until closing time. Just because I was fifteen minutes late getting back from lunch on Tuesday you want to make an example of me. How about some of the executives? Look in their offices between noon and two o'clock. Nobody there. I work just as hard as anybody. You know as well as I do that people in this office don't expect to be hassled for being a few minutes late. With the subways the way they are, people come in at all hours. When you do something about them, let me know. Don't pick on me."

What should personnel director Worthington do in such a situation? Put in a time clock? Have a meeting with supervisors to try to tighten things up? Should she pick out some of the worst offenders in the office and begin to discipline them? It is an age-old problem. Anyone who finds a solution will win the "personnel director of the year" award by acclamation.

Punctuality became a social necessity during the industrial revolution, which required the integration of many tasks. Thousands of workers had to carry out their functions at exactly the right time for the system to work. As America devotes itself less to industrial production and more to service and communications, the emphasis upon punctuality may recede. Flextime and optional work schedules will become more common. Nevertheless, lateness will continue to be a reason for discharge for many employees.

In a factory, employees punch a time clock. Foremen control the comings and goings of the people on the floor. When lateness occurs, it is amenable to prompt and effective discipline.

THE CHRONIC ALCOHOLIC

Alcoholism and drug addiction are major causes of absenteeism. Punishment may not correct the behavior. Nevertheless, discipline may be helpful. An important factor in dealing with alcoholics is getting the worker to recognize the problem and to seek help. To the extent that discipline signals the depth of management's discontent, it may persuade the employee to do something about the problem.

According to a recent Conference Board study, an increasing number of corporations are using "shape up or be fired" programs to deal with alcoholic workers. They are treating alcoholism as an occupational problem rather than a medical dilemma. Job performance is the key. The study covered over thirteen hundred companies. It reported that personnel departments are removing the problem from medical units and are concentrating on the employee's work-related failings. The technique is called "constructive confrontation." According to one expert, "the threat of losing one's job is said to be the most effective motivation for getting the alcoholic to treatment." Workers who refuse treatment run the risk of being fired.

Alcoholism is viewed as a serious problem by 72 percent of the companies surveyed. Many alcoholics find it difficult to hold jobs. Alcoholism and overindulgence of alcohol is a common cause of termination. Just as other illnesses sometimes excuse poor work performance or absenteeism, alcoholism may be grounds for mitigation. But management's tolerance need not be boundless. The mere claim of addiction will not excuse poor work performance.

Arbitrators have taken various positions as to alcoholism. As a general rule, a grievant must prove that he is trying to cure himself of the problem. Where convinced that the person is seeking help, arbitrators have reinstated workers, sometimes contingent upon completion of a rehabilitation program. Other arbitrators have sustained discharges on the theory that management cannot afford to expose other people to danger by assigning an alcoholic to a high-risk job. Who wants to load cargo under a drunken crane operator?

The chronic alcoholic presents special problems. A recent discharge case at American Enka illustrates some of them. The individual had been with the company for many years. The company knew that he was an alcoholic. A supervisor called the grievant on his day off, giving him an opportunity to work the midnight shift as a replacement for an employee who had called in sick. The grievant showed up drunk. He collapsed on the floor near the time clock, incapable of punching in. The company discharged him. The arbitrator put him back on the job: "Dismissal under these circumstances must be considered disciplinary overkill." The drinking took place at home. The grievant had not expected to work that evening. When he was invited to work, he should have declined but the alcohol probably impaired his judgment. This was different than drinking before a regular shift. The employee never did punch in. The plant rules prohibited bringing liquor into the plant or consuming it on plant premises. Those actions would have required immediate dismissal.

Alcoholics are a problem for themselves as well as for their employer. But what kind of problem? Does an alcoholic intend to get drunk? What weight should be given to attempts to reform? How should progressive discipline be applied in such cases? What mitigating circumstances should be considered?

One woman was refreshingly candid when I talked to her after she lost her job, "Let's face it: I was a lush. I was pretty good at my job. I could finish up everything in the morning. At twelve, I took off for one of the nearby hotel bars. When everyone else was eating lunch, I was getting smashed. That happened every other day for several years. I couldn't understand why nobody said anything about it. I was good at hiding it but surely they must have known. Finally, one afternoon, they called me into an emergency meeting with one of my clients. I fell asleep. Then the fat was in the fire. They had to confront the fact that I was drinking myself to death. They gave me a couple of chances after that, but by then I was pegged as a problem. It wasn't worth the hassle. When they asked me to leave, I left."

Alcoholism is an illness, with a residual element of free choice. One labor arbitrator has said that the important issue is whether an employee can be saved. Some managers would disagree. As they see it, an alcoholic who is unable to give up drinking has no place in the working world.

How should an employer treat the long-term worker who gradually becomes an alcoholic? What obligation must be assumed to help such a person survive on the job?

In a labor arbitration case in a cement plant owned by National Gypsum, the company tried to help an alcoholic resolve his health problems. The situation continued to deteriorate. The grievant had thirty-three sick days in his final year, during which he suffered four seizures while at work. Finally, he was discovered unconscious, lying in a precarious position across the top of the cement mill. He was given an ultimatum. He would shape up or be fired. The company registered him in a course of treatment for alcoholism. The grievant failed to complete the program or to attend AA meetings on a regular basis. He was fired. The arbitrator was sympathetic, but the employer had been "very patient and did exercise extreme forebearance." It could no longer provide a safe and efficient workplace for the grievant. He sustained the discharge.

An employer must be consistent. One firm embarked upon a crusade to stamp out drinking. An employee came to work completely drunk. The testimony indicated that he "staggered, waved his arms, slurred his speech, rolled on his heels, and smelled of alcohol." He did not deny that he had been drinking. The company fired him. The union argued that discharge was too severe a penalty. Other employees had been given warning letters, three-day suspensions, and demotions for being drunk. Why was this man discharged? The arbitrator found that the employee was fired as part of a new "vigorous compaign against the ravages of intoxication." The arbitrator held for the grievant, without back pay.

How About Drugs?

The presence of nonalcoholic drugs among the workforce is a contemporary phenomenon. What an employee does on his own time is generally thought to be his own business. But when drug usage impinges upon job performance, the employer may take appropriate action.

A custodian in a public school came to work after taking a medicine called Darvon, prescribed by his doctor for an earache. He seemed disoriented and sluggish to both the area manager and the school principal. His speech was slurred. His walk was unsteady. His movements were slow. They told the man to go home. When he refused, he was fired for reporting to work "under the influence of alcohol or drugs." Darvon causes drowsiness and impairs mental abilities. The grievant was reinstated.

Recently, discipline for smoking pot has been deemphasized. A Swift & Company employee was caught by one of the plant guards smoking a reefer in the washroom during his lunch break. He was discharged for violating the plant rule against using drugs on company premises. The arbitrator reinstated the employee, without back pay, on the theory that smoking marijuana is no longer the kind of misconduct that calls for discharge on the first offense. "A rule prohibiting drug use in the plant is certainly reasonable. The company clearly has the right to expect its employees to report for work and to remain in a state of mind which will enable them to produce the company's product in a safe and efficient manner." The employee had a good work record for eight years. The company had not warned the employees that they would be fired for smoking pot. "It can no longer be said that a rule prohibiting the smoking of marijuana during lunch break, without elaboration, gives notice to a first offender that he will be discharged."

The management of a California factory hired a detective to find out whether employees on the third shift were using narcotics or alcohol. According to the agent, one worker sold him some marijuana. The employer discharged the worker. The penalty for possession of narcotics on company property was termination. The union was outraged when it learned of the undercover operation. It claimed that the company should have notified it in advance. The arbitrator pointed out that if the union had been told about the operation, it would have had to warn its members. The grievant denied having sold marijuana to the agent. The arbitrator was convinced that the agent was telling the truth and decided that the discharge was justified.

In a similar case, an arbitrator refused to credit the uncorroborated evidence of an undercover agent. "To hold otherwise would be to allow guilt to be created by an undercover agent acting alone and reacting to his own likes and dislikes. While the testimony of the agent seems forthright, it must fall if it stands alone." Each of the grievants denied the charges of selling marijuana and liquor and charges of bringing prostitutes into the premises. The company had not reported the situation to local law enforcement authorities. According to the grievants, the company was trying to get rid of a group of black employees on the second shift. The agent's report was not corroborated by either direct or circumstantial evidence.

Undercover operations are a nasty business. When surfaced, that tactic seems repugnant to employees. Most workers think that management should not use spies, and become angry when they are exposed, a heavy price to pay for catching an occasional drug dealer.

FIGHTING

Some of the most dramatic discharge cases are based on violence at work. Fighting tends to be more common in the rough-and-tumble atmosphere of a factory than in offices or retail shops where employees are in contact with the public.

The impact of such behavior on the business is the important element. The world of work brings together people with varied personalities, who are together five days a week. Fights must be avoided. Employers recognize that they have a duty to create a safe and productive atmosphere. Employees who disrupt the working environment are likely to be disciplined.

A similar issue also arises when arguments break out between employees. So long as the arguments do not disrupt the work, they may be tolerated by the employer, or they may form the basis for minor penalties.

Fighting causes more concern. It will usually bring down disciplinary action, often against both participants. If one of the antagonists shows that he acted in self-defense, his penalty may be mitigated. The severity of the penalty depends on company policy and its past practice in administering punishment for similar incidents.

CHALLENGING SUPERVISION

If a worker threatens a supervisor, the employer must respond. When supervisors give orders to employees, they expect them to be carried out quickly and efficiently. Compliance is essential. Management cannot tolerate a direct challenge.

A union member is expected to carry out a supervisor's order. If he believes that the orders are unjust, the grievance procedure can be invoked as the method of protest. The rule is "obey now, grieve later." Employees who refuse to follow a direct order may be disciplined for insubordination.

Anything that threatens the supervision's authority is likely to lead to discharge. Some examples: assault upon a supervisor, using abusive language towards management, insubordination, refusal of a job assignment, refusal to work overtime or disloyalty to the employer.

Only in a most unusual case will an assault upon a foreman be condoned, either by management or by a labor arbitrator. One exception involved the discharge of a young man at the Pen Foundry Company. He worked as a mold tender, shoveling sand from around the machines. While engaged in that work, he was asked to go down through a hole in the floor to bring up some wooden pallets. This task usually was given to other workers. It was a particularly bad assignment. The area under the floor where the pallets were kept was overrun with rodents, racoons, and snakes. The last time the grievant went for pallets, he encountered a rat and announced that he would never go there again. He told the foreman that he was behind in his work and pointed out that several other employees were standing idle. The foreman insisted. When the grievant continued to refuse, the foreman discharged him. At that, the grievant lost his temper and struck the foreman several times.

This was a small company. Several members of the grievant's family worked there, including his father and brother. It was the grievant's brother who pulled him away and calmed him down. The arbitrator pointed out that in 99 cases out of 100, a discharge for striking a supervisor is sustained, but "arbitration . . . does not ignore the prevailing circumstances." This grievant and his relatives were all excellent employees. Based upon the mitigating circumstances, the grievant was put back to work by the arbitrator.

INSUBORDINATION: PROVOKED?

Management demands loyalty and expects that its orders will be carried out. When an employee challenges a supervisor, the power and authority of the management group itself is being threatened. These situations frequently result in immediate punishment. Management will take prompt action. Employees should bear this in mind when called on the carpet for some minor deriliction. If a worker argues with a supervisor, one word may lead to another, ending in a charge of "insubordination," which may result in dismissal.

Insubordination may arise from an incident provoked by a supervisor. For example, a fork-lift operator was told several times to help fix some broken machinery. He continued driving around on his vehicle. The foreman swore at the operator, calling him a "wetback Mexican." The worker climbed down from his fork-lift and struck the foreman in the chest with his fist. An arbitrator put that man back on the job: the foreman had provoked him. Would you agree?

Many insubordination cases involve situations where none of the participants are entirely free from blame. During an argument, the supervisor may have provoked the grievant. In non-union shops, employees may be more likely to knuckle under when faced with such treatment. Top management may never find out what really happened. Or they may learn about the incident to their embarrassment many years later in federal district court, after the victim has filed a lawsuit.

UNION ACTIVITIES

The challenge to management may be organizational rather than personal, a work stoppage rather than assault. The fact that an employee is acting as a representative of the union may protect him from being disciplined. The National Labor Management Relations Act prohibits reprisals against "committeemen, stewards or union members because of their union activities on behalf of their fellow workers."

Sometimes a union badge can act as a shield. An employer may be reluctant to convert an individual grievance into a major confrontation with its union. One of the American Arbitration Association's training films presents such an issue. Called "All

Things Considered: The Case of the Militant Shop Steward," it shows the precarious position of a shop steward: protected, but also a lightning rod for employer hostilities.

Special considerations are raised in discharge cases that involve union officials. For example, engaging in an illegal strike, personal misconduct during a strike, or participating in an organized slowdown may lead to discharge. The law does protect employees against being fired for union activity. But a shop steward should be sure that the activity is covered by the law. It may not be enough for a grievant to say that he was acting on behalf of the union. The law does not condone misconduct that goes beyond legitimate union activities.

The company must convince an arbitrator that it was not attempting to rid itself of a union activist. In one case, a furniture company in Cincinnati proved that the grievant, a shop steward, had told one of its customers that the company "always screws their customers—they sell nothing but junk." Even so, the arbitrator held that the company had failed to demonstrate that it did not discharge the man because of his union activity.

A dramatic example of a union official exceeding the limitations of his position occurred recently in a valve factory in Louisiana, where a black shop steward tried to force seven Vietnamese employees to join the union. Over a period of several months, he threatened several of them, slashed the tires on their cars, and even stuck a pistol in one worker's back. The Vietnamese were frightened and finally left the company. The employer fired the shop steward. After a full review of the facts, the arbitrator upheld the discharge.

The relationship between labor and management is usually maintained on a businesslike basis. In one recent incident at a feed mill in Springfield, Illinois, that was not the case. The union president, who was employed as a fork-lift operator on the third shift, happened to meet the plant superintendent in the company parking lot. He accused the superintendent of having lied during a committee meeting. He threatened to shoot him with a shotgun that he had in his car. The superintendent ran for his life toward the office building. When he came to the door, he screamed, "Open up the door. That son of a bitch is going to shoot me." Earlier, the grievant also had threatened the assistant superintendent, showing him a live shotgun shell and telling him that he would blow his head off and splatter him all over the office wall. The company called the police and hired Pinkerton guards for security. The president of the union was discharged over the telephone. The plant superintendent, who had been with the company for twelve years, quit and moved to another city. An arbitrator upheld the discharge: "An industrial operation is a miniature society involving a number of people working at various levels with different duties and responsibilities. It will operate successfully only if unacceptable behavior and actions are removed. This must be done for the welfare and job security of all."

Other cases have demonstrated that it is permissible for a union steward to call a supervisor a "liar" or a "fool." As long as such language does not interfere with the operation of the plant, such insults or profanity may be part of the normal process of labor relations. Such language will not support a discharge.

When a worker is fired by a nonunion employer for trying to organize the other workers, an unfair labor practice charge can be filed with the National Labor Relations Board. According to former *New York Times* labor reporter Abe Raskin, over ten thousand charges were filed with that agency in 1974 by employees dismissed for union activity. The backlog of the N.L.R.B. and the delay in its deliberations are notorious, but it is the only game in town for a nonunion worker who has been fired for trying to organize his co-workers.

Unions are not winning as many organizing campaigns as they used to. Some very sophisticated consultants have become available to fight off unions. Unfortunately, the individual workers who get caught in the cross-fire between the company and the union are often the sacrificial victims in a battle to organize. Once discharged, they run the risk of being blacklisted in their community. "The worst thing that ever happened to me was attending that organizing committee meeting. My name was reported to management. From then on, I couldn't do anything right. I went through the progressive discipline steps like a log going down a chute. I was out in two months and the union never did organize the company."

PERSONAL BEHAVIOR

When employees are fired for something they have done while they are off the job, arbitrators tend to be skeptical of the employer's motivations. The employer must be able to demonstrate that the action prejudiced its business interests.

Many arbitration awards have stated that what employees do at home is their own business, as long as it does not hurt the employer's reputation or economic interests. Employees have the right to engage in social, community, and political activities of their own choice.

It is in this area that educated, newly liberalized workers are most vociferous: "When I leave the office, it is my life again. Whatever activities I choose to engage in, whatever controversy I involve myself in, whatever notoriety I achieve is my problem and should be no concern to my employer." That is what a young woman asserted after being arrested for picketing a 1980 speech by a Republican presidential candidate, on behalf of a womens' rights organization. After lengthy internal discussions, the corporation that she worked for agreed not to discipline her.

She was lucky. In a similar case, involving a telephone company, an employee was fired for his involvement in a civil-rights demonstration. After litigation in the civil courts, the discharge was upheld. The company was not required to demonstrate that the young man's activities prejudiced its business. If it did not like his behavior, it could fire him.

Sometimes, testimony about personal behavior becomes pertinent to a discharge for on-the-job misconduct. A Transit Authority bus driver in Akron, Ohio, was fired for molesting a twenty one-year-old woman who was the sole passenger on his bus at 5:45

A.M. She claimed that while she was riding on the bus, the driver stopped in front of a shopping mall and turned out the lights. "Let me show you what an old rooster can do for you," he said, and attempted to kiss her. When she complained about the incident some six days later, the "old rooster" was fired, even though he had a good work record prior to the incident. The manager of the bus line testified that he was aware of a prior incident involving the driver's sexual advances to a woman, which took place while he was off duty. The arbitrator upheld the discharge.

Early-morning bus riders can take comfort in the arbitrator's opinion: "The employer cannot maintain in its employ a driver who sexually assaults a passenger alone in his bus in the dark hours of morning."

SEXUAL HARASSMENT ON THE JOB

Employers are no longer tolerant of sexual harassment. A recent incident at the St. Regis Paper Company plant in Vernon, California, indicates how management is likely to react in the present climate of opinion.

The grievant had been working as a wastebaler on the graveyard shift for about one year, during which time he had already received warnings for poor performance and absenteeism and had been suspended for aggressive conduct toward a supervisor. The incident for which he was discharged took place as a result of an argument that he had with a nineteen-year-old female janitor, during which he poked her in the chest with his finger, spilling some Coca-Cola on her clothes. She threw the rest of her Coke at him and kicked him in the leg. Shortly afterward, he came up to her and said, "I'm going to get you. I'm going to rape you." She reported him to management. He was fired.

At the arbitration, the woman testified that on three earlier occasions the grievant had handled or grabbed her against her wishes. The grievant denied everything. The union attributed the charges to the woman's "sheer vindictiveness." But the arbitrator upheld the discharge. "She was not willing and was not obliged to tolerate a threat of rape."

It can be expected that employers will no longer acquiesce to such behavior. They know that they can be held liable if they condone it. They will hand out heavy penalties in harassment cases.

OFF–DUTY CONDUCT

Airlines sometimes discipline workers for off-duty conduct which they believe is harmful to their image. Where an employee is not working or wearing the company uniform, such discharges are likely to be overturned. For example, one Air California employee was terminated for "streaking" in front of the Los Angeles terminal at the end of his shift. Not grounds for discharge, said the arbitrator, the grievant obviously was not wearing the company uniform.

When the grievant's off-duty conduct does not harm the employer's reputation or interests, render the employee unfit for duty, lead other employees to refuse to work with him, or undermine management's ability to direct the work force, a discharge will not be sustained.

An off-duty employee who had been drinking drove his motorcycle through the plant and back. He was discharged. The arbitrator pointed out that "even while off-duty, an employee is under obligation to refrain from acts or conduct which would detract from the company's image and may have a harmful effect upon the company's role as an employer and its managerial authority." Nevertheless, the arbitrator reduced the penalty to a two-week suspension without pay, viewing the incident as horseplay rather than a malicious act.

Employers cannot punish workers for their behavior outside of the plant unless that conduct has an impact on the employer's business. There must be a business connection. An employee can be disciplined who moonlights when forbidden to do so by the employment agreement. But an employee cannot be fired for not using the company's product.

Arbitrators require a high standard of proof in such cases. The employer must be able to show that its business interests are being prejudiced by the activity.

Nonunion companies are likely to be less finicky. One executive was beaten up outside a homosexual bar. The incident was kept out of the newspapers, but he was asked to resign. Whether he could have won the case in court if he had been fired will never be known. He moved to another city and found work in a different industry.

Another employee, an engineer for one of the nation's largest chemical companies wrote a novel that described a similiar company that bilked engineers out of patent licenses and was unfair to its professional employees. After the book was published, he was fired, but he sued the company for damages.

The situation has improved since the days when public-school boards could require unmarried teachers to live in domitories. In general, arbitrators and courts have drawn a line between performance on the job, as contrasted with the personal life of the employee. But non-union employees still act at some risk when they violate the employer's cultural standards.

Fundamental questions are involved. How much of an employee's life does management own? An employee should not assume that his personal life is entirely insulated. Decisions as to promotions or pay increases may be made on the basis of subjective considerations. In many corporations, the employee's family life will be taken into account when management makes career decisions. These considerations would not be appropriate grounds for discharge: for other purposes, they may be weighed by an employer. When the image of an employee is tarnished by extraneous personal factors, subjective judgments may result that could not be justified on more objective grounds.

The chief executive of one major corporation put it this way: "Our management group is based upon decent Christian values. I can tell you that no young man has a chance in this company who has not demonstrated that his attitudes and life style are harmonious with our point of view. I don't care how able he is or how energetic and well qualified he may be, if we are not convinced that he will fit into our pattern, he has no place in this corporation.

I asked him how he felt about "alternative life styles." "Don't get me started on that. I am not saying that I would fire one of our people who started messing around with that stuff. But I can assure you that neither I or any successor that I could visualize being asked to run this company would promote an officer who did not have respect and concern for traditional family values."

An employee's reputation may be based upon factors that have little to do with job performance. An employee's career may rise or fall on such judgments. It is important to know what criteria management had adopted for its employees. If applied consistently, they may shape the internal value structure that insures job security. An employee is well advised to identify such standards and to accommodate to them. For example, management at IBM is said to prefer that executive employees dress conservatively. The rule may seem arbitrary, but a well-paid executive commented that an IBM employee could do worse than to follow the guidelines.

Certain work rules are listed in the employee manual or posted on the walls of the shop. Other rules, while unstated, but may provide equally important clues to operating successfully within the company environment. Sometimes such rules must be learned by example or picked up through casual observations of co-workers. If your boss makes a snide remark when someone comes to work in a turtle-neck shirt, it doesn't take a genius to realize that casual dress is not being encouraged by management. No one may get fired for ignoring the code, but when it comes to a promotion, a turtle-neck shirt, loafers, and long hair may weigh heavily against the offenders.

Considerations such as these would not constitute just cause for discharge. Personal biases, subjective evaluations, and caprice would not impress an arbitrator. For that very reason, the just-cause standard may be rejected by a boss who prefers to make decisions on the basis of how he feels about a person. That is understandable. It is equally understandable that some people do not like to work under the threat of arbitrary and capricious discipline. Many younger workers have come to believe that they should maintain their full legal rights while they are working.

They expect fair treatment. They would like to have the same rights and privileges on the job that they have as citizens. Such attitudes are becoming increasingly common.

For example, a guidance counselor in a public school made the mistake of confiding to one of the secretaries that she was bisexual. The secretary told the principal. A meeting was called to deal with the problem. The guidance counselor attended with her attorney and a representative of her teacher organization. The school board was represented by the principal, the school superintendent, and the board's attorney. The latter took over the meeting:

"We called the meeting to ask for your resignation," he announced.

"On what grounds?" asked the guidance counselor.

"It has come to our attention that you claim to be a lesbian."

"That's all?" asked the guidance counselor's lawyer. "My client needs time to consider the situation."

"I won't resign," the guidance counselor blurted out.

"In that case, you are suspended. Don't report for work until further notice." For the rest of the year, the grievant worked in limbo, assigned to writing a training proposal, with no contact with students or other teachers. In the spring, she received a letter of nonrenewal. So far, she has found it impossible to get another job in the schools.

Life-style cases are interesting because they indicate how much of our identity must be mortgaged to our job. When someone is discharged for reasons that have nothing to do with work, the termination-at-will doctrine seems particularly repugnant.

When a woman is fired because she refuses to sleep with her boss, or when an office worker loses his job because he will not lobby against cigarette smoking, or when someone is terminated for being a homosexual, one has to wonder about the fairness of the system. What are the rules of the game? The next chapter will describe the current law and practice of employee rights. Can a worker be fired? How is it done?

4

The Rules
of the Game

YEARS AGO, UNDER AMERICAN COMMON LAW, an employer had the absolute right to discharge an employee for whatever cause he might choose, without incurring liability. Employees could be terminated at will. It was a harsh rule, born in the hard-knuckle days when workers were regarded as a commodity to be purchased or rented as business required.

What an old fashioned idea, you may say. Not at all! For many workers and their bosses, it represents the current rules of the game. Termination at will remains very much alive in its most absolute form in a majority of states. Even today, most American workers can be fired arbitrarily. If you are fired tomorrow, there may be nothing you can do about it. Even employees who have put in years of service may be discharged for no reason at all.

Some sophisticated management lawyers advise their clients not to give any reason when they discharge a worker. "Just tell them they no longer have a job. That is the cleanest way to get rid of them. Tell them that they are through. Don't get into a discussion about your reasons." Some American court decisions seem shocking, based on naked economic power. Even where the employer has been brutal, courts may support the action. The common law was clear: unless an employee could show that the discharge violated a specific statute, a worker could be discharged at any time, for any reason, without legal recourse.

David W. Ewing describes a "typical" firing in his book *Freedom Inside the Organization*. It goes like this: the worker is called into the boss's office. He stands alone, facing two management representatives. His immediate supervisor is not there. One of the executives tells him that he would be better off somewhere else. It would be sensible for him to leave voluntarily, with a severance payment and good references. If the worker objects or asks questions, he is told that the offer may be withdrawn. They refuse to give him anything in writing.

- The employee is alone.
- The atmosphere is coercive.
- The reasons for discharge are vague and undocumented.
- There is no opportunity for the employee to confront supervision.
- Nothing is put in writing.
- Severance payments are non-negotiable.

It adds up to a picture of a corporate bully tossing out human garbage. No wonder some workers leave with the feeling that they have been brutalized. Firing should not be done that way in a free country.

Our common-law doctrine was formulated by employer-dominated courts during the early days of industrial capitalism. It was a harsh economy then. The common law of master and servant is still harsh. Our free country can be a harsh country. In the words of the United States Supreme Court, it was taken for granted that "either party could terminate an employment relationship for any or no reason" (*Geary v. U.S. Steel Corporation*).

A Utah court later bragged that "under our system of free enterprise and individual freedoms, there is no serfdom." There may be no serfdom, but there are plenty of nervous employees.

Earlier, it had been assumed that employment was by the year, unless otherwise agreed. Employment could be terminated only after reasonable notice, unless there was good reason for canceling the relationship. In an 1849 case, *Truesdale v. Young,* a pilot on the Hudson River was fired without cause. A federal court upheld the discharge. An "industrial" theory of employment crept into the national law. Laissez-faire attitudes toward workers began to appear in court decisions.

In 1877, a law professor named Horace Gay Wood published a textbook on the "Law of Master and Servant," popular with the employers of his time. He confirmed the termination-at-will doctrine.

> With us the rule is inflexible, that a general or indefinite hiring is prima facie a hiring at will, and if a servant seeks to make it out a yearly hiring, the burden is upon him to establish it by proof . . . . It is an indefinite hiring and is determinable at the will of either party, and in this respect. there is no distinction between domestic and other servants.

After the new rule was accepted by the New York courts in 1895, it was adopted by other courts throughout the United States. Termination at will became embedded in the law: "The most fundamental rule of the law of master and servant is that which recognizes that, absent any applicable statutory or contractual provision to the contrary, an employer enjoys an absolute power of dismissing his employee, with or without cause."

A worker could not question a discharge. The employer was not required to provide a grievance procedure, or do anything more than point toward the gate. No importance was attached to the employer's motive. He could give a reason for the discharge or not give a reason. In any case, the employer was not required to show that his reason was justifiable.

In 1908, in *Adair v. United States,* the U.S. Supreme Court justified the rule on the grounds of mutuality. "The right of the employee to quit the service of the employer, for whatever reason, is the same as the right of the employer, for whatever reason, to dispense with the services of such employee." The court argued that it would violate the Fifth Amendment of the Constitution to compel an employer to retain the services of an employee. It would be "slavery."

Does the logic of the Court seem odd? Don't despair: your confusion commends your common sense, and your humanity. Justifiable or not, "mutuality" became well entrenched in the law. The Civil Code of Lousiana still retains the flavor: "A man is at liberty to dismiss a hired servant attached to his person and family without assigning any reason for doing so. The servant is also free to depart without assigning any cause."

Legal scholars came forward to justify the rule on theoretical grounds. Several pointed out that the employee had paid nothing for job security. Workers were free to come and go. Wasn't it a free country? No employee could be forced to work. That would constitute involuntary servitude. Hadn't the Civil War just been fought over that issue?

The Termination at Will Doctrine Still Lives

In *Geary v. U.S. Steel Corporation,* a salesman had been fired after fourteen years of service. He claimed that he was being punished for telling his superiors that the steel tubes the company was selling were defective and would be dangerous in high-pressure installations. After he communicated his misgivings to a top sales executive, the company took the tubes off the market. But he was fired. The Supreme Court of Pennsylvania dismissed his suit. "The law has taken for granted the power of either party to terminate an employment relationship for any or no reason." Many other cases endorse the same principle.

American employees are at risk. When the economy turns rotten and business is bad, jobs are anything but secure. The employee can always quit. In bad times, because of limited job skills or advanced age, there may not be a hope in hell for that worker to obtain another job: but the employee can always quit. Therefore, an employer has the right to terminate without notice. Got it? Mutuality.

The rule was born in harsh times. Back then, judges were adept at verbalizing why economic interests had to be protected against the rights of mere individuals. Even now, an individual employee who goes to court may regret it. Being involved in a lawsuit is time consuming, expensive, and frustrating. Lawsuits between employees and their former employers can be tough. Corporate employers resent being sued. They may make sure that the plaintiff does not get another job in their industry. Corporations have long memories.

As one elderly claimant was advised, "I don't like to discourage you, but unless you can afford a lawyer, forget it. They won't do a damn thing for you. Get yourself a good lawyer. That's the only way." Not many discharged workers can afford to hire a good trial lawyer, which is one more impediment to using the courts.

Suing an employer takes time. Under our system, after a case is filed it is usually necessary for the attorneys to interview witnesses under oath. This process is called "discovery." Only when that has been completed can the case be set for trial. It is not unusual for an employment case to be in preparation for several years before trial. Then, if the employer loses, the grievant can expect an appeal, which can take more time. Those are hard years.

Employees do not get much comfort from the reported cases. In the case of *Edwards v. Citibank,* the bank fired one of its thousands of executives. He claimed that he had uncovered evidence of illegal foreign-currency manipulations. He said that he was being punished for acting in the public interest. Edwards had been employed for six years. He said that the bank's employee handbook was like a contract. It gave him a permanent position, terminable only for cause. Justice Martin Evans rejected that theory. The handbook was not a contract because it did not "completely define the terms and conditions of employment." Retaliatory firing was not actionable under New York law.

Edwards was a "whistle blower." In recent years, laws have been passed to protect employees who report improper business practices. Truth in lending, fair credit reporting, equal opportunity, environmental protection, and foreign corrupt practices statutes are examples. These anti-reprisal rights are not well known, even to lawyers. But corporations are aware of them, and may be cautious about punishing employees who act under their protection.

American managers argue that employers must have the right to terminate workers. Most Americans believe that the right to fire lazy or unproductive workers is an important part of the free-enterprise system. We exist in a competitive world. The right to terminate unproductive employees is necessary in order to maintain an efficient workplace, one that is beneficial to both the investor and to hard-working employees.

When Is an Employee Not an Employee?

The American economic system includes many workers who are not employees. Employment is the most common working relationship, but, in our innovative society, individuals work in other capacities: as partners, providing their services under a contract of allegiance; as independent contractors, where a firm purchases services without controlling the work; as franchisers, who agree to operate under the guidelines of the enterprise; as grantees, where a government agency or foundation provides funds for a certain project; as volunteers, who accept supervision, but receive no financial compensation; or as students, where the work is supposed to provide a learning experience.

Each form of "employment" has it's own termination problems. The partner, the independent contractor, and the dealer look to their contract in the event of a cancellation. When a dealer is terminated, the event may look exactly like a firing, and may have the same sting. Dealers and franchisers in some industries have lobbied for protective state legislation.

Volunteers and student interns share some of the problems of employees. Legally, they can be terminated, but a trustee of one hospital told me that her board dreaded having to terminate nonproductive volunteers. "Sometimes, the entire board of trustees gets into the act when one of our elderly, volunteer benefactors has to be terminated. Some of these women have served the hospital for years. They give money. They know everybody. They love the hospital. Getting rid of them means a real battle."

Another catagory of worker is the housewife. Her importance is chronically underestimated. When described in terms of replacement value, the housewife becomes economically visible. It takes many thousands of dollars a year to replace her. When the family has been raised and the working cycle completed, the housewife finds herself in a precarious, perplexing position. Will she be "laid-off" by her husband, now that she has completed her service to the family? When the nest is empty and the breadwinner announces that he is dallying with Ms. Assistant Buyer in the big city, the plight of his spouse as a redundant worker comes into sharp focus. Can she be fired? Until modern times, the law regarded the wife as the husband's servant. Vestiges of that notion still exist. The law now gives a divorced wife more security than it gives most workers, assuming that the husband/employer is willing and able to pay. Which he may not be!

How Much Security Should a Worker Expect?

The larger question is whether people who have devoted themselves to an enterprise, giving it their loyalty and their productive capacity, should not receive employment security in addition to temporary benefits of compensation, dignity, and a sense of belonging. Certain Japanese workers, mostly males in large corporations, enjoy an employment relationship for life, or at least until they are fifty five. Is that a useful model for America, the arsenal of freedom?

I was recently warned by a top executive in a major industrial firm to get my priorities straight: "We are in a life and death struggle with the rest of the world. They are running all over us with cheap labor, government subsidies, and a sense of discipline that we haven't had in this country for three generations. Unless Americans are willing to bite the bullet and accept some hardship, the game is lost.''

Most American executives claim the right to dispense with employees who will not do as they are told. There is no more basic credo in the executive manual. In the words of one plant manager: ''Management means control. Unless we have the power to direct the organization and to fire people who won't follow orders, there is no way that this company can operate. I am all for being sympathetic and learning as much as I can about what's bugging my people. But where the rubber hits the road, management must have the final say.''

Our courts have supported management, enforcing the right to discharge employees. Traditionally, an employer had no obligation to give any reason for discharging a worker. Employers could simply say, ''You are fired because I don't like you.'' This approach may be risky. Certainly, it is not recommended. In Chapter 2, I encouraged supervisors to have a good reason for the termination and to be sure that the law is on their side. The employee will expect an explanation. The action should not come as a surprise. If things are not working out, the worker should be warned. Otherwise, the terminated employee will feel that the boss was unfair.

A secretary in a brokerage firm expressed this view: ''Why was I fired? I don't have the slightest idea. Sometimes my boss would get very angry and scream at me: afterwards, he always apologized. Then, he would be very careful to explain things. When I made mistakes, I could tell that he was trying to be patient, to control himself. Lately, he hasn't been shouting as much. I thought that I was doing better. He should have said something.''

Many workers do not realize how totally unprotected they are. They understand that members of unions may be put back on the job by an arbitrator. Somehow, they assume that they have the same protection. In this, they are quite wrong. Millions of American workers are not covered by civil service or by union contracts and have almost no legal protection when they are fired.

In practice, their position may not be as precarious as the case law might lead one to believe. Many employers exercise restraint. A large nonunion corporation is well aware that it's employees have the option of organizing, so many firms try to provide exactly the same rights that a union would demand. The company wants to persuade employees that they do not need a union. Wages and benefit programs may be just as good, if not better, than they would be under a collective bargaining contract. Absence of job security is the one major difference. That lack provides a sales point for a union organizer: "You are not protected. You can be fired if your supervisor does not like you. Only my union can protect you."

Nonunion employers try to demonstrate that employees have nothing to fear, by exercising restraint, by adopting progressive-discipline programs, and by providing formal grievance procedures. Even so, whatever job protection nonunion workers may have is granted at the pleasure of their employer. What the employer has given may also be taken away. Termination at will is a fact of working life.

A Survey of Corporate Termination Practices

I asked my research associate, Paul Salvatore, to investigate how major American corporations terminate nonunion employees. Paul is a good interviewer. He talked with personnel executives from many fields, including broadcasting, banking, and transportation. He used the roster of the New York Personnel Management Association. The members of that organization are active in personnel administration at the management level, with titles like personnel manager, director of personnel, or vice president, personnel. Their corporations employ thousands of employees. They have responsibility for planning, organizing, and directing their company's personnel program.

When Paul made a call, he explained that he was studying non-union discharge procedures for this book. Some people refused to be interviewed: it was "against company policy" to talk about such things. "We do not discuss our policies with outsiders." Others said that they were too busy to meet with Paul or did not return his calls. Fortunately, some were willing to talk. A few asked that their anonymity be protected, obviously nervous about discussing the subject of discharge. They thought it strange that anyone would want to investigate the topic. Others seemed ill at ease. As one executive explained, "it is very unpleasant to sit across the desk from somebody you've known and worked with, and tell them that they are fired. I'm even uncomfortable just talking about it."

Another reason for embarrassment is that for these professionals each discharge represents a failure. One handbook for managers puts it like this: "An employee is a valued resource, an investment to be developed and protected . . . . Stability of employment is a valued objective. Every reasonable effort should be made to retain employees. Efforts to minimize separations should receive high priority."

Companies dislike having to terminate a worker they have recruited and trained. It is a mark of failure, particularly for the personnel director.

Reasons for Discharge

Salvatore asked each company to list the reasons why an employee might be fired. Those grounds are usually specified in the personnel manual. For example, one corporate personnel handbook lists five reasons:

1. Unsatisfactory attendance/punctuality
2. Unsatisfactory performance

3. Lack of qualifications
4. Changed requirements of position
5. Misconduct

Where not listed, the reasons for discharging an employee tended to be more subjective: "unsatisfactory performance," "wrong person for the job," "cutbacks," "behavior problems," or "lack of potential."

Every personnel executive interviewed said that there had to be a reason for discharge, using terms such as "cause," or "just cause." When asked if there was some legal obligation to show that good cause for discharge existed, several said that they had a moral obligation. Others claimed that they felt a "self-imposed" or "implied" obligation. "Based on recent court decisions," one employee relations manager said, "we must have a good reason to fire somebody, and be able to prove it." When challenged, they denied having any legal obligation to prove just cause. The extent of their responsibility was to justify the necessity to themselves.

Termination Procedure

No two termination procedures were alike. In a sample of twenty firms, eleven firms had formal procedures covering all employees, irrespective of job title. These procedures were based on progressive discipline. Six firms had formal termination procedures covering all employees except managerial personnel, based on progressive discipline. Three firms operated without any written procedures.

Some companies professed to be even-handed, applying the same procedures to every employee. One respondent put it this way, "We believe in blind, dogmatic enforcement of our discipline policy. The same rules apply to a stock boy or vice president." Other firms have quite different standards for various categories of workers.

Progressive Discipline Procedures

In the case of a failure to perform, most companies rely on progressive discipline, described by one respondent as "a necessary practice due to the nature of everyday human chemistry." The procedure involves several steps:

1. counseling
2. written reprimands
3. final warning, with a probationary period
4. dismissal

During the preliminary steps, the company will try to rehabilitate the employee. A typical corporate policy:

When separations are initiated by the company due to the employee's inability or unwillingness to perform satisfactorily, the following procedures are applicable:

1. COUNSELING

A counseling session with the unsatisfactory employee may be the best way to correct a situation. Postponing counseling may lead to continuing failure. The manager should assume that the individual wants to be a productive employee and will correct any faults, given proper guidance. Counseling should be instructional. The manager should show a genuine interest in identifying and correcting the cause of the unsatisfactory performance. In most instances, no further action by the manager will be necessary.

2. WRITTEN REPRIMAND

Any reprimand should be in writing. If the unsatisfactory performance has not been corrected by counseling, the written reprimand should emphasize the importance of the situation, describe the particular deficiency, review any previous discussions on the subject, define the standards of performance that are expected, and specify a period of time to correct the deficiency.

The consequences of the employee's continuing failure to maintain satisfactory performance should be noted: deferral of salary increase; lack of promotional opportunities; possible loss of job. The manager should give a copy to the employee. A copy also should be placed in the employee's personnel file. The manager should fix an appropriate follow-up date to determine if improvement is achieved. If the employee subsequently achieves a satisfactory level of performance, an appropriate memo should be placed in the file.

3. FINAL WARNING

In giving a final warning, a manager should make it clear that the responsibility for remaining rests entirely in the employee's hands. The final warning should contain the following elements:

1. Copies of previous written warnings.
2. Specific areas in which the employee must improve.
3. A period of time within which to correct the unsatisfactory performance.
4. A statement that this is the final opportunity to bring performance up to the required level. Continuing failure will result in the employee being terminated. A copy of the warning should be given to the employee and placed in the personnel file.

If the employee corrects the unsatisfactory behavior, a memo should be prepared by the manager indicating that the employee is removed from final-warning status on the understanding that the acceptable level will be maintained. A copy of this should be given to the employee and placed in the file. If unsatisfactory behavior recurs, the manager should decide whether to issue a new final warning.

4. DISMISSAL

Before concurring in a termination, the department head should determine that the employee is not meeting performance standards established for the job, has been informed of such shortcomings and counseled on the improvements required, and has been warned that dismissal will result if performance does not improve. The manager supervising the employee is responsible for informing the employee of termination.

Severance pay is designed to provide economic support until new employment is secured and is provided on a discretionary basis. It is not earned or accrued during employment. The amount is determined by the department head, after consultation with the personnel department.

Comments on Corporate Procedures

The personnel executives who were interviewed by Salvatore made the following comments about their company's procedures:

- "Our termination policy, because it is so formalized, protects the rights of employees by ensuring their access to due process. A final warning letter is a birthright of our employees."
- "I'll try anything before starting down the road of progressive discipline. Transfers, demotions, you name it. Management has an investment in an employee, you have to give it your best shot."
- "Under our system, except in cases of gross misconduct, an employee should know it's coming. He has to. There is too much give and take between employer and employee."
- "Ours is a policy of discussion and written documentation. In the case of a performance deficiency, employees should know the areas that they are deficient in, what it is they must

do to become adequate, and how long they have in which to do it."

- "The intent of any discipline policy, especially ours, is to improve performance, not to get rid of an employee. We can go only so far. Once the employee is placed on final warning, it is up to him. The ball is in his court." [It is interesting that personnel directors often talk in sporting terms.]

- "The objective of a discipline procedure is to turn around deviant behavior. Working with an employee, not just putting him on probation and saying 'Boy, I've got him nailed.' The manager should try to help the employee."

- "When an employee is having problems, we'll set up an improvement action plan in the early phases. This serves as a guideline to better job performance."

- "I am always reminding our people that they must be careful in administrating the steps of progressive discipline. An employee may feel he's being badgered rather than helped along the road. You have to maintain a balance. You don't want the 'pull the trigger' syndrome, but neither do you want deadwood lying around."

- "You have to realize that employees are an investment. Not all of our managers realize this. As investments, you should treat employees like capital equipment—carefully, respectfully and helpfully." [Treat us like people, not machines.]

- "Taking care of an employee means taking care of his employment rights. Employees have rights, just like the company has rights. Our policies, I hope, reflect a balance of the two."

- "Talk about gross misconduct, we had one ticket agent who lent out his ticket validator to a friend. That is equivalent to giving away free tickets. We suspended him on the spot. When dollars and cents are at stake, human values sometimes get pushed to the back of the line" [an airline.]

- "With some employees, all the training, counseling and remedial help in the world isn't going to work. They're misfits. All you can hope to do is to move the employee out of the organization with some degree of self-respect.''

One firm, in its discharge procedure for clerical employees, had the most rudimentary system of all.

1. Supervisors should, whenever possible, give the employee the reason for discharge in writing.
2. A copy of the reason for discharge should be given to the department head.
3. Two weeks notice or two weeks pay in lieu of notice is not required.

Special Procedures for Executives

Executives are often treated differently than lower-level personnel, not necessarily more sympathetically. Some companies demand complete loyalty. As the director of personnel for a leading drug manufacturing company was candid enough to say, ''In this outfit most executives cling to the belief that lower-level managers work for them. They demand personal loyalty. They're like generals in the field who expect their lieutenants to obey them, no matter what.''

Executives may be excluded from the company's grievance procedure. This often occurs in broadcasting, fashion businesses, or publishing, where top management wants to be able to discharge executives quickly because of the volatile nature of the industry. ''In this business, dismissal of managers can be sudden,'' a labor relations director with a publishing concern reported, ''Things change too fast. Executives are expected to perform. If they don't, they know the consequences. The results of poor performance by an executive are too devastating.''

A top executive in a broadcasting network explained why many top people were being dumped. ''It is the ratings system. Our people live or die by the ratings. They understand it. They are paid well while they last. When they get the heave-ho, they take some heavy bucks with them."

This is not to say that executives are fired capriciously. Many firms have policies requiring a higher level of management to approve the discharge of any manager. That policy was defended by one personnel vice president: "Executives have many perks and privileges. One thing they do not have, in this industry, is job security. It does take two levels to fire them."

Firms have special ways of firing executives. Some use management by objective, a technique for establishing performance goals and holding the manager to achieve them. The comments of personnel executives in this connection were candid:

- It's a matter of personality. You can't handle executives by the book, especially creative people. (publishing)
- With most executives, if you do your homework, you don't have to fire them. If you lean on them hard enough, you get a voluntary resignation. (banking)
- We use a case-by-case method when dealing with our upper-level personnel. We tailor our actions to a person's problems. We don't believe in formalization for the sake of formalization. (insurance)
- With managers, there are what you might call "gentlemen's agreements." When someone upstairs gets the axe, down here in corporate personnel, we are the last to know. (textiles)
- The higher you go, the harder it is to establish measureable standards of performance. Executives deal with complex problems. The standards they're measured against are more abstract. Sometimes they are so abstract, they boil down to whether the boss likes them. (broadcasting)
- You don't discipline executives. You care for them and feed them. If they don't perform, you get rid of them. (retail)

- I had a very close friend who was a manager and got fired with no prior warning. She was just called in and dismissed. I saw what she went through. It would have torn your heart out. It came down to a personality problem. Because of this and other incidents I've seen, I'm a big advocate of some kind of warning. Talk to them. Lay it on the line. If they can't handle it, that's their problem. I'd be mortified if I was fired without some sort of prior notice. (advertising)

Three firms had no formal policy covering the discharge of nonunion employees. They said that they applied standards similar to those required for employees covered by union contracts. "We apply the same rules," one personnel manager said, "but we haven't told our people that that's what we do." None of these firms had a special procedure for the termination of managers.

Several firms claimed to be working on new, formal procedures. "We've been able to skate along like this until now," one personnel director remarked. Another said "Due to the paternalistic nature of our firm, we've not needed a formalized policy . . . but in light of the social and regulatory climate that exists today we'd be better off having one." He sounded frustrated.

Role of the Personnel Department

In general, personnel departments play an indirect role in the discharge of employees, "advising and counseling managers and ensuring consistency of application." "We can tell them how to proceed but we don't make final decisions," said one personnel vice president. Another, paraphrasing Gertrude Stein, emphasized that "the line is the line is the line. The final decision to hire and fire an employee must always rest with the line manager."

An important duty of the personnel department is to educate operating managers, so that they understand company policy, especially the progressive-discipline system. The key is trained supervisors. Most large corporations maintain in-house training programs. These programs are often run by the personnel department. Their goal is to teach "people" skills to managers, including how to fire an employee.

Despite existing programs, many personnel directors say that managers need help. "We don't provide enough training for managers," one complained. "We'll go into an accounting department and say 'you're the best accountant and you're going to be our new manager—responsible for salaries, transfers, EEO, everything.' Do we train him? Not enough!"

"If our managers only had to deal with pieces of paper and machines, it would be heaven," said another. "We must constantly remind them that they are managing people, not paper or machines."

When it comes to discharging people, the lack of training is apparent. Over and over again, people tell me about managers who have fired people in the most insensitive of ways, stripping them of their pride as well as their job. It seems so unnecessary.

Discharge Resulting in Claims of Discrimination

In recent years, the role of the personnel department has grown because of the increasing number of discrimination charges. "We become involved in these situations because of their potential explosiveness." The personnel department monitors what would normally be the supervisor's duties, making sure that decisions are correct.

Another personnel manager said, "With minorities, we are very careful to document every action taken by the company. These cases are dynamite. Our executives have learned to call us in early because many of them have already burnt their fingers."

Legal proceedings are time consuming and expensive. A case described by a personnel vice president for a major textile firm tells the story:

> One of the reasons companies are becoming very meticulous about discharges, especially where there are possible discrimination overtones, is that you can't win these things. For example, we discharged an employee. He ran down to the Department of Labor. They told him to take a hike. Then, he initiated an action with the New York State Commission on Human Rights. They held a hearing and determined that he had no case. From there, he went to the Appellate Division. They rejected his appeal. Finally, we found ourselves in federal court. After he lost there he finally dropped the case. Hurray! We fought that discharge for over two years and spent an enormous amount of money and time, $140,000 in legal fees alone, winning in every forum. We are not anxious to go through that again.

Personnel directors dislike lawsuits and try to avoid them wherever possible. The cost to the company can expand when an individual case becomes a class action. For example, a group of women filed an action against Chase Manhattan Bank for sex discrimination. The bank was able to settle, for a price. Chase had to agree to eliminate sex discrimination, insuring that women had total access to jobs. In addition, it agreed to invest $850,000 in recruiting females into the bank, training supervisors to understand the equal employment opportunity law and its enforcement, and providing career-development seminars and counseling. A half-million dollars had to be set aside for incentive payments. The plaintiffs received $229,000. Their lawyers got $145,000 for legal fees and costs. Even for a major bank, these are substantial sums. Management would prefer to install such programs on it's own initiative rather than be forced to do so by an abrasive outside attorney.

Nor are successful claimants always pleased with the result. One woman involved in such a victory is still bitter:

> They bought us off. We have career programs and the men are more circumspect, but nothing, really, has changed. Women are still outsiders. When the guys take off their spikes at the golf club and sit around having a cold beer, we aren't there. They know it and we know it. Without Title VII, we would be pounding typewriters. With it, we get to go to meetings. We hang around the men who make the decisions. We have a long way to go.

The Open Door and Other Internal Remedies

What appeal procedure is available for the employee who gets fired? Will the decision be reviewed by top management? By an impartial third party? All twenty companies surveyed had some form of appeal. Thirteen had formal grievance procedures. Six had "open-door" policies. One had a grievance procedure ending in arbitration. The open-door policies were in nonunion paper factories, like banks and insurance companies. It was claimed that they encouraged "open, comfortable relations between supervisors and employees."

United Airlines has a procedure for nonunion employees including managers, which, in the event of discharge, gives the employee a final right of appeal to "two top officials of the company to be designated by the Chairman." These executives must review the original decision and report directly to the Chairman in writing.

Personnel executives in some companies admit that employees rarely use the open door in discharge cases. "I guess the employees view it as a management gimmick."

Employee handbooks usually describe some procedure; very

informal; a place to complain, and a willingness to discuss problems; nothing binding. There is no obligation to observe just cause, no impartial review. An excellent analysis of nonunion grievance procedures is contained in Fred Foulkes' *Personnel Policies in Large Companies,* recently published by Prentice-Hall.

Some of handbook verbiage is almost inspiring:

- The open door policy is deeply ingrained in the company's history.
- The company cannot emphasize too strongly its desire that all company people shall feel free to call attention to any condition that may appear to them to be operating to their disadvantage.
- You . . . are encouraged to resolve any differences. You are encouraged to make use of these procedures.
- Employees are completely at liberty . . . to bring the matter to the attention of anyone in management.
- Our policy provides that every employee be treated in a fair and just manner at all times. All employee complaints shall be given full consideration.

Usually, grievance channels lead to a top manager. Foulkes thinks that these programs can be effective if the executives, in practice, carry out a thorough review and investigation.

A procedure must be trusted before it will be used. Some employees may suspect that the open door leads to the back door, that a complainer will be marked as a troublemaker, that supervisors resent any use of the procedure. In order to eliminate such perceptions, management must support the process. A supervisor must be reversed from time to time to demonstrate to employees that the procedure works.

One firm encourages employees to let the personnel department "do the talking," while appealing their case to successively higher levels of management. The personnel director described a situation where an employee was fired soon after being transferred. Her new job required her to work closely with the supervisor while being trained in the complexities of the new position: "They told me that they fired the woman for not being able to do her work. She said that she was fired because she was pregnant. Her boss had said 'Why should I train you and then just have to train someone else when you leave.' We reinstated her after an investigation."

Trans World Airlines Arbitration System

Trans World Airlines maintains a nonunion grievance procedure ending in arbitration. The company believes that its employees appreciate being able to obtain an impartial review of supervisors' decisions.

- Our procedure has been in effect since the 1950's. Our union employees have always had these provisions in their contracts, so I guess it's only fair our nonunion have the same rights. Some employees are afraid to use it—others think it is terrific.
- We in personnel play a neutral role in this process. Personnel used to present the company's case against the employee. We dropped that a few years ago because it put us at odds with the employee. We try to promote the idea that personnel has a two-handed role, although employees don't always see it this way.
- Grievants often are confused. That is why we hope they will trust personnel enough to allow us to explain the system to them in an impartial way.
- The discipline imposed by this system is good for everybody. It makes employees and managers sensitive to each other's rights.
- Managers view this procedure as an infringement on their rights. Some are more enlightened than others, but most never get over that attitude. If someone files

a grievance, it reflects on them. They don't want the grievant to win because they feel it will somehow show that they did something wrong.

To obtain an outsider's view of the system, Paul Salvatore attended a TWA arbitration hearing. The case involved poor work performance. The following memo had been placed in the employee's file:

This letter is to confirm our discussion of October 30 regarding your lack of adherence to standard jetway operating procedures which resulted in damage to an aircraft. On October 29, you retracted the jetway from an aircraft without first making a visible check to insure that power cables were not still attached to that aircraft. Your failure to do so caused the cables to be pulled taut and bend the receptacle pins. As you stated, you are aware of the proper procedure and are an experienced jetway operator. You will be re-briefed and re-certified in jetway operating procedures. If you are in need of any further training or assistance, please feel free to contact me or any other Field Manager.

The grievant admitted his error but did not think that his work record should be tarnished. He had been with TWA for twelve years. The board members included a member of management, a representative of personnel, and a co-worker picked by the grievant. Salvatore was permitted to attend the board's discussion of the case. The board unanimously voted to uphold the disciplinary action. Salvatore thought that the procedure was fair since the grievant had admitted a fairly serious infraction.

The TWA procedure is also used for discharge cases. In one case, a personnel clerk was discharged for adding fictitious overtime to her own payroll record. The errors were picked up by a spot check of the audit records. She was terminated by the passenger service manager, based on a company rule that "no employee shall knowingly submit inaccurate or untruthful information on any company record." The grievant testified that she had always been an honest employee. She was not responsible for the discrepancies and did not know who was. In a sixteen-page opinion, the arbitrator upheld the company. He pointed out that the TWA grievance procedure was established to assure that the policies of the company are applied in a fair, reasonable, and non-discriminatory fashion. He said that he would "follow the common law of grievance arbitration, that body of doctrine which has been developed by arbitrators in ruling on discharge grievances arising under collective bargaining contracts."

When the discharge is based upon dishonesty, the employer must prove by clear and convincing evidence that the employee engaged in the alleged conduct. An employee discharged for dishonesty is likely to have difficulty obtaining another job. That is why a heavy burden of proof is justified. The arbitrator reviewed the testimony of the grievant and compared it to the copies of the payroll record. He found inconsistencies which persuaded him that the grievant was not telling the truth: she had filed false payroll records. Since she had been entrusted with maintaining such records, there was just cause for her discharge.

We discussed voluntary arbitration with other companies. Most personnel directors expressed interest. Some were skeptical. Others claimed that their employees did not want it. Another personnel director indicated that he had been suggesting arbitration for years. "Companies had better realize that people have the right to know where they stand. Most labor attorneys and union officials claim that discharge is capital punishment. It's the electric chair. I agree 100 percent. Think how you would react to being fired. You're dealing with a human life. Humans make mistakes. That's why people should have the right to arbitrate."

How Important Is Having a Union?

Many supervisors in nonunion corporations seem to be misinformed: they believe that "just cause" is already the established policy of their employer. They think that they must conform to that standard. Either management has neglected to tell them about its "union-free" environment or their misunderstanding indicates a change in cultural perceptions. Some recent court decisions, described in Chapter 5, suggest that just cause may become the rule for nonunion workers.

Most individuals must fend for themselves in negotiating for a job. You hear about a job, interview for it, and accept it on a take-it-or-leave-it basis. Some high-powered executives are able to obtain individual employment contracts to protect themselves against being fired. Most job applicants don't have that power and can't make that good a deal.

Some workers protect themselves by electing a union to represent them in collective bargaining. But union members are only as strong as their union, and some unions are not very strong. A union's weakness may appear in various ways. Some can only afford to take a few cases into arbitration, which can be an expensive process. Union leaders may make concessions on some cases to get settlements on others. A union's weakness also can show up at the negotiating table. Salary increases may not keep up with inflation.

Almost every day one reads of plant closings where thousands of workers lose their jobs. Particularly during a recession, when an industry is losing ground with foreign competition, the union may be unable to keep employers from closing plants.

In the construction industry, a union member works only when the union can find an available job. When business is slow, there may not be enough jobs to go around. Union members may have to do nonunion work or work off the books.

Even civil-service employees, thought to be the most secure of American workers, have been caught in recent budget cuts. The tax crunch on some urban communities has resulted in job reductions. This deterioration in municipal government payrolls has influenced the job attitudes of the public worker. Government workers are protected against dismissal by civil-service laws which provide elaborate systems for appeals. Also, the courts require government employers to abide by due process when an employee's rights are involved.

As one government lawyer told me, "Working for Uncle Sam has one great advantage. I can say what I think. I play agency politics with impunity. If I don't like what's coming down, I bitch about it. Sometimes I'm tempted to take a job with business, but I don't want to have to knuckle under to keep my job. Here I can be my own man."

Rank-and-file government employees feel free to criticize the policies of their employer. In a landmark case, an Illinois high-school teacher accused the local school board of spending too much money on athletics. She was fired: the Supreme Court upheld her right to speak out. Like other taxpayers, school teachers have the right "to comment on matters of public interest."

Total Job Security: Slumberland

In some socialist countries, the workers do not seem much concerned about serving the public. Is this caused by too much job security? Or are lax supervisors unable to motivate the workers? Everyone has a job in the system and no place to go. To an American, accustomed to the prompt and friendly service of private airlines personnel, it seems intolerable to stand in line for more than an hour to check-in for a flight, as I had to do in Warsaw last year.

Dealing with government workers in the United States is not always pleasant. Obtaining a driver's license in New York City, an unemployment check in Los Angeles, or a public-welfare voucher in Chicago may dispel any notion that people work harder if they have job security.

In one recent arbitration case, an obese municipal inspector in Iowa City was fired for sleeping on the job. The city learned that the employee was literally eating himself to sleep. After a suspension, the city took him back on the job, with the understanding that he go on a diet. Unfortunately, the grievant continued his overindulgent eating habits. He would consume dozens of soft drinks and candy bars at his desk. Caught sleeping again and again, he ignored the city's warnings. He was fired. An arbitrator concluded that the grievant was at fault. "The presence of an employee asleep at his desk is not conducive to a public image of an efficiently operated city. Other employees . . . become dissatisfied and disgruntled. The morale of these employees is directly affected by this condition which occured in their view and in the full view of public patrons."

Unfortunately, some public employees become so bored that they learn to sleep with their eyes open. Taking revenge upon the public, they carry out their duties in slow motion, disdainfully doling out licenses, forms, and benefit checks at a leisurely pace. Some managers believe that only the threat of discharge will activate such employees. Perhaps. But the employer may be at fault, denying them an opportunity to participate in the work. They become alienated. The threat of losing their job will not increase their interest in their work.

Employees seek personal dignity, a sense of belonging, friendship, and other benefits. They need to be supervised in a positive and progressive fashion. Most workers expect fair play, some degree of job security. Many are shocked to learn that they can be fired without cause, that they work at the pleasure of their boss.

The Problem of Layoffs

In our economic system, managers are held accountable for short-run profits. When sales decline, they are expected to cut costs. Layoffs accompany business recessions. Lost jobs are the carnage of the private employment market. The layoff problem is handled differently in other developed countries. There, the government is likely to intercede to protect workers threatened with layoffs.

This difference in approach can be illustrated by General Motors' response to a declining market for automobiles in the United States and in Germany. When sales declined in the United States in early 1980, more than 130,000 hourly workers from GM's American plants went on indefinite layoff. In Germany, the market also suffered a decline, but the GM subsidiary, Adam Opel AG, was under coordinated pressure from the government, from works councils, from worker representatives on the board, and from the German press. The company was forced to negotiate a voluntary separation program. When sales declined 19 percent in the first four months, the company had to persuade 2,300 workers to take early retirement even with a year's pay. Voluntary resignation was also offered to about 3,000 younger workers, who would receive bonuses ranging from $3,693 to $7,102. The balance of the firm's 65,000 German workers continued to work. Even then, German labor leaders complained that they felt frustrated and powerless.

Under American labor contracts, seniority determines who will be dismissed. Newly hired minority and female workers often bear the brunt of the layoffs. Some employers would like to devise some alternative to layoffs by seniority. They don't want to lose ground on their equal employment goals.

One black leader put it in eloquent terms when he said, "Seniority is the last vestige of slavery. You tell my people that they have equal opportunity and then, when things get rough, you kick them out of the plant."

Spread the Work Plans

It has been suggested that the burden of lay-offs be spread over the entire work force. Everyone would work a short week.

Unemployment compensation insurance would pick up the balance. That approach is favored by Eleanor Holmes Norton former head of the Equal Employment Opportunity Commission. She would like to see state unemployment laws amended to encourage such programs.

A pilot program in California has involved hundreds of employers. Perhaps some such system, supplemented by an unemployment subsidy, will be devised to ease the pain of economic cutbacks. A similar arrangement can be devised for white-collar workers. According to the *Wall Street Journal,* one company, Aero-Quip of Libbey-Owens-Ford, did that in May of 1980. Instead of laying off surplus salaried workers, it gave them work for four weeks followed by one week on unemployment compensation. By rotating time off, the company was able to maintain its staff.

According to Gail Rosenberg of the National Council for Alternative Work Patterns, rotation is a good short-term solution. It keeps employees on the payroll, maintains affirmative action ratios, and makes it possible to continue the fringe-benefit package. Any such scheme has to be designed to accommodate to state unemployment insurance. And even if new formulas are devised to deal with the problem of temporary economic layoffs, millions of American employees will continue to be laid off when business is bad.

Critics say that the American attitude toward layoffs is inhuman, inappropriate for an enlightened and wealthy society. But many executives believe that termination at will is a legitimate price to pay for an economy that provides a high rate of production. They argue that business must have the flexibility to move capital from one industry to another. They note that the American worker's freedom of job opportunity is envied throughout the world.

America is a land of opportunity where it is possible for an able, hard-working, and fortunate person to become wealthy and successful. For the employable individual, the enterprise system can be rewarding. That is the bright side.

Harry Maurer's book *Not Working* contains conversations

with people at unemployment insurance offices around the country. These people, the losers, testify to the dark side of the American employment system. Maurer described some of the victims, such as a thirty-four-year-old father of three who was laid off by American Motors from the job that supported his family: he became totally demoralized. Week after week he sat around, gained twenty pounds, watched television, felt lazy and irritable. He complained that he was restless from the time he got up until the time he went to bed.

A middle-aged woman in an insurance company was fired. She "felt a little retaliation was in order," filed a complaint with the Fair Employment Practices Committee and went to work for the union trying to organize the company. She became an angry labor organizer.

Maurer describes people who have been victimized. Some have suffered but survived. Others have taken action against the system. For some, being fired was a blessing: they found better jobs. Others were clearly victims. As a result of his interviews, Maurer expressed a profound distrust of American society. He concludes that the American system is inhuman.

Full Employment

A full-employment policy might be more humane. But as Maurer points out, America does not seem ready for full employment. In 1945, Congress declared that "all Americans able to work and anyone seeking work should have the right to useful, remunerative, regular full-time employment." Government would create enough jobs for everyone. Thirty-three years later, Congress passed the Humphrey-Hawkins bill, a pale reflection of the original concept. The reality of full employment is far away.

Business leaders oppose full employment, believing that it is alien to free enterprise. They defend the right of private industry to hire and fire at will.

Being unemployed is a common experience. Increasingly, Americans work for large organizations. As corporations wax and wane, consolidate and liquidate, large numbers of workers and executives are shuffled off the workforce. Employees who are quite capable of doing their jobs become surplus. In times of recession, hundreds of thousands are laid off as a result of plant closings.

So many people are unemployed, it is surprising how few organizations have been established to represent their interests. A few groups have been formed, like 40 Plus, to help find jobs. But no powerful lobby has evolved to change the system. The anger of the unemployed worker is diffuse.

American industry defends its right to close unprofitable operations and dismiss workers. Some firms pay generous severance benefits to soften the blow. But the principle stands: employers have the right to lay off workers when business is no longer profitable. A plant closing can cause enormous human suffering. As the ex-president of one local union said, after a shutdown cost him his job, "I think the day is long since past when, in a civilized society, a company can just up and move their plants without any regard for the workers and the communities." His own plant had been closed on Thanksgiving Day, a few days after management thanked him for his members' cooperation and high productivity for saving the business. He was outraged!

On the other hand, a state that adopts laws making it more difficult to close unprofitable plants may seem inhospitable to corporate investors who don't want to be locked into a hopeless situation. Such legislation could be the kiss of death to a state's economic growth plan.

Bills to regulate plant closings are pending in several states: New York, Ohio, Pennsylvania, Michigan, Illinois, Indiana, Massachusetts, and Rhode Island. Similar legislation is being considered by Congress. These bills are sponsored by manufacturing unions concerned about losing members in impacted industries and by communities who are worried about local unemployment. They would require corporations to give advance notice before closing plants and to provide indemnity payments to the community and to provide transfer rights for workers. Management will lobby against such laws. Audrey Freedman of the Conference Board thinks that such laws have the effect of "ossifying present industrial structures.'' Nevertheless, plant-closing laws may pass in states that suffer heavy job losses. Wisconsin already requires severance pay to impacted workers.

What to Do About Productivity

Unions believe that the responsibility for maintaining productivity belongs to management. It is not up to the union to force a company to modernize. Even where an economic crisis is obvious, the union may refuse to help. Sometimes, management itself seems unwilling to confront the problem until it is too late. Then, nothing can be done except to close the business. Too late, employees realize that they no longer have a job.

Until recent times, management discounted the ability of workers to participate in solving production problems. Only trained engineers and consultants were considered smart enough to help. This is changing. The employees who do the work may be the best experts.

Sometimes, in order to save their jobs, workers have purchased a plant that would otherwise have been closed. Why do they wait until the moment of crisis? Couldn't they see it coming? Early cooperation between the union and plant management could lead to greater job security.

Increasingly, the heads of international unions are recognizing the need to improve productivity. Robert A. Georgine, president of the Building and Construction Trades Dept of the AFL–CIO, put it this way: ''We fully recognize the benefits that higher productivity can bring workers, and we are ready, willing, and able to pull our weight.'' This spirit has not always been shared by less enlightened local union leaders; but the interest in labor-management cooperation seems to be growing.

Georgine has emphasized the important contribution that can be made by individual workers.

Workers bring a tremendous source of knowledge and experience to their jobs and the operations of the business for which they work. Tapping this source of expertise can yield tremendous benefits in terms of new ideas and concrete suggestions for improvements, ranging from technical improvements in machinery to new ways of organizing an office.

Even in the best of working relationships, most executives believe that the power of management to supervise the workforce must be maintained. Sometimes, this notion is expressed in terms of ownership. "I don't give a damn," one owner said, "It is my business. I started it. I'm the one who is going to run it. It is my money. You think that the people who work here have anything to say about my business? Forget it. The trouble with this country is that nobody respects property any more."

Some Thoughts on Human Dignity

Holding a job in America can be scary. The employment market can shift suddenly, without warning. Workers may be terminated for no good reason. The United States has a higher rate of unemployment than most other developed countries. The growth of our national economy has slackened. Inflation has encouraged a tight job market. Jobs are not equally distributed. Other countries have developed more effective programs for retraining workers, with more protection against layoffs. Full employment has become a strong part of their political commitment.

When people are subjected to high rates of unemployment, they may question the economic system. Throughout history, there have been hardcore unemployed, people who cannot find work or cannot hold a job because of poor health or lack of education. When, to these groups, are added substantial numbers of employable people who are unable to find work, ingredients for radical change in the system may be simmering.

Into the United States in recent years, have poured millions of unemployed immigrants. These people are eager to accept jobs that Americans might disdain. They increase the pool of available labor.

Periods of high unemployment tend to diminish human dignity. When large numbers of job seekers become available, employers place a lesser value on the individual. An employee who doesn't produce can easily be replaced. High salaries can be demanded by people with unique skills, but workers who are only interchangeable parts in the production process can't make such demands.

Sometimes employers resent the fact that workers are not robots. "We make these elaborate plans. Then it turns out that somebody didn't get the word. Nothing works the way it should. The human factor can kill you." But employees are people. They come to a job with human weaknesses and strengths, with feelings, emotions, personal needs. The cases in this book show what happens when real people rub against each other.

When there is a labor surplus, employers have less patience with the "people" inside their workers. Who needs a problem when there are dozens of other workers who can do the same job for less money?

American employers are not expected to keep workers on the payroll when there is no work to be done. Many people believe that management's duty to the enterprise requires that the workforce be reduced when business is bad. In times of recession, layoffs will continue to occur. People will lose their jobs. Traditionally, in America, unemployment insurance has been the major political response to the layoff problem. Unemployment benefits provide a safety net for people who get fired.

The Unemployment Compensation Solution

Even before the turn of the century, some states had established relief programs for poor people who were unable to find jobs. Usually, recipients of such assistance were required to perform some public service in return for being supported. Private charity also helped. Then came the Depression. As one oldtimer recalls the situation, "You either found a job or you were out in the street. It seemed like every other person was out of a job. When I graduated from college, I would have taken any job. I mean any job! I will never forget how hungry I was in 1930."

When chronic unemployment set in, the level of support was inadquate. A few states responded by enacting unemployment insurance legislation. The Wisconsin law became the model for the unemployment insurance provisions passed by Congress as part of the Social Security Act of 1935. The act encouraged every state to create an unemployment insurance system. At the time, it seemed unlikely that a federal program would be upheld by the courts. It seemed safer to require state-administered systems. The individual states were given broad latitude to establish their own programs within federal guidelines. A tax was levied on payrolls. By 1937 all of the states had enacted unemployment insurance laws and were in compliance with federal standards. Coverage, eligibility requirements, benefit amounts, and the duration of payments were fixed by the state.

Most industrial and private office workers are now covered. Over 80 percent of the states cover state and local government employees. To be eligible for unemployment benefits, an applicant must have earned qualifying wages during a specified period, must be available to work, must be seeking work, and must be free of certain disqualifications. The laws vary in detail. The aim is to restrict benefits to unemployed persons who are separated from the labor force involuntarily. In order to qualify for such benefits, you must file a claim and register for work at one of over two thousand local public-employment offices. If you are found to be qualified, benefits will be paid.

Much of the case law has to do with disqualifications. For example, a worker who quits a job without good cause may be ineligible. If a worker is discharged for misconduct, about half of the states will deny benefits for a fixed period of time. If a worker refuses to accept a suitable employment offer, benefits may be cancelled. Other disqualifications are based on the fact that an applicant is not available for employment, is already employed, or quit the prior job voluntarily.

A former employer will sometimes contest an application, seeking to protect its experience rating. But one of the benefits of the system is that the contest is between the applicant and the state fund, not directly against the former employer. There is seldom a direct confrontation between the worker and his former employer.

A typical case involving misconduct:

A registered pharmacist in California failed to report for work because he had been put in jail on a charge of illegal possession of narcotics. After he was released on bail, he confessed to his employer. He was dismissed from the job, and was later found guilty and sentenced.

The appeal board concluded that the claimant was discharged for misconduct. "We are of the opinion that the claimant's illegal possession of narcotics was an offense which was so closely related to his occupation with the employer as to destroy his suitability for employment as a pharmacist in the employer's establishment." The claimant did not qualify for benefits and the employer's account was not to be charged.

Another case from California:

The claimant worked as a bellman in a hotel. One evening, he was asked to provide room service by an intoxicated female guest. He claimed that he remained in her room for no more than five minutes, discussing her marital problems. Later, she called the desk to ask for a bottle of liquor. When the claimant delivered it, she invited him to have a drink, which he did. More time was spent discussing her personal problems. In the morning, the guest claimed that her purse was missing. The hotel manager reprimanded the bellman for drinking and spending time in a guest's room, but fired him for theft, which was not proven. The board held that the claimant was discharged for misconduct. Benefits were denied.

An arbitrator might not have upheld that discharge. There was no proof that the hotel had any rule against drinking with guests in their rooms. The guest was an unreliable witness. The manager gave false testimony as to the reason for discharge. In the absence of a bad record, a labor arbitrator might have returned the bellman to work.

The following unemployment insurance cases, from New York, Wisconsin and Pennsylvania, are typical:

- A young woman left her job for lunch and did not return until the following day. She had received previous warnings about being absent. The New York Appellate Division confirmed the Appeal Board's findings of misconduct.
- An automobile salesman refused his employer's request to pick up a car that had been sold. He was discharged. Again, a finding of misconduct.
- A general manager of a marina and pleasure-boat agency failed to open for business at 9 A.M. on Saturday as instructed. He didn't show up until 11 A.M. In the meantime, the president of the firm drove past, saw workers and customers waiting, and opened the store. He discharged the general manager.

In a lengthy opinion in the latter case, a Wisconsin Circuit Court upheld the Appeal Board's determination of willful misconduct. Under the Wisconsin statute, misconduct is defined as "willful or wanton disregard of an employer's interests." The court noted that the claimant had been a good manager, was knowlegeable about boats and had good relations with the customers. The man's salary had been reduced from $20,000 to $12,000 because of poor business conditions. Judges in Wisconsin have often tempered the zealous enforcement of the unemployment insurance department. In this case, the court upheld the board's disqualification of the claimant.

- In Pennsylvania, the operator of a press drank beer with his lunch and also took a pain pill for a minor ailment. The combination made him so dizzy that he collapsed on the floor while trying to operate his press. The company prohibited drinking or taking medication while on duty in the press room. He was fired. The state board found willful misconduct. The court affirmed the decision. Benefits were denied.
- More than a decade ago, Shirley Zinman lost her job as a secretary for an employment agency. She had been told to secretly record telephone conversations with prospective clients. The office manager wanted to listen in. Shirley thought that was illegal and quit. The Pennsylvania unemployment board refused her application for compensation. With the backing of the ACLU, she contested the ruling. A state court upheld her right to quit. The decision was hailed as an important victory for workers' rights.

Some of the cases that come before state unemployment insurance boards are similar to grievances heard by labor arbitrators under union contracts or to claims heard by industrial tribunals in other countries. The facts may be substantially the same, but the legal issues are different.

- Under unemployment insurance, the board decides whether the claimant is qualified to receive benefits from the state fund.
- In labor arbitration, the arbitrator must decide whether a grievant was discharged for just cause, and if not, whether the grievant should be reinstated with back pay.
- In most other countries, a government tribunal will decide whether a discharged worker should receive compensation from the employer.

One clear advantage of unemployment compensation is that an individual worker is not forced to confront the former employer. The person who has been fired and the person who did the firing are not forced to fight with each other. The employer may challenge the worker's eligibility for benefits, but not as a direct party to the action, as would be the case in arbitration or before a labor court. Lawyers seldom appear in unemployment insurance proceedings. It is not worthwhile.

The amount and duration of unemployment insurance benefits will vary from state to state. For example, a worker with no dependents may receive $90 per week in Mississippi, but $202 in the District of Columbia. In most states, the maximum potential duration of benefits is twenty-six weeks.

During a recession many workers exhaust their unemployment benefits. In 1970, Congress extended unemployment compensation to pay up to thirteen weeks of additional benefits.

In most states, unemployment insurance is financed from employer contributions. Under an experience rating system, an employer can reduce its tax rate by keeping claims to a minimum. Employers may try not to fire as many workers. Not a bad idea.

Some unemployed people exhaust their benefits before they are able to obtain a new job. They have fallen through the safety net. Other workers manipulate the system, working just long enough to qualify for benefits or maintaining themselves with off-the-books income while they exhaust their coverage.

Although the unemployment system can be criticized, it is nevertheless, our primary mechanism for protecting workers who have lost their jobs. It has some unique advantages. By its ingenious design, it maintains the employer's right to terminate workers, but places the burden upon all employers to support workers while they look for another job.

The basic unemployment insurance system, supplemented by the extended compensation system, supports over eight million people. Additional protection to unemployed workers with unusual political clout has also been provided. For example, the United Auto Workers have negotiated supplemental unemployment benefits with the major American auto companies. These programs provide up to 90 percent of the worker's take-home pay for the first year of unemployment. The burden falls upon the industry.

A federal subsidy, the Trade Adjustment Assistance program,

pays benefits to workers whose jobs have been lost because of import competition. The cost has grown to over a billion and a half dollars. Other special unemployment programs cover federal employees, military personnel, and postal workers. These groups represent strong lobbies. Together, these programs contribute many millions of dollars to our federal deficit.

Unemployment insurance raises an important political issue. To what degree do we wish to subsidize unemployed workers? Should such support be provided through general taxes or by placing the burden on employers? Can we continue to maintain unemployment compensation programs? The original concept of unemployment insurance was that the burden would be shared by all employers. Recently, the general taxpayer has been assuming an increasing share of the burden.

A National Commission on Unemployment Compensation issued a comprehensive report on the system in 1980. Chairman Wilbur J. Cohen pointed out that the only alternative to strengthening unemployment insurance would be "more far-reaching revisions and drastic changes in the . . . system." One such change might be greater restrictions upon employers' right to terminate workers. "The volatile and corrosive effect of uncompensated unemployment can cost society much more than the cost of a reasonably improved unemployment compensation system."

The Commission recommended strengthening benefits by exempting them from taxes, eliminating the adjustment against pension income, and opening up eligibility to new categories of employees. The level of benefits would gradually increase from 50 percent of average salary in 1983, to 65 percent after 1989. A recommended supplementary program would provide up to twenty-six weeks of additional coverage. Part-time workers would be included in the program. "Family obligations" and "sexual harassment" would be added as legitimate reasons for employees to quit. A solution to the problem of the displaced homemaker was also recommended. Other recommendations would give additional protection to older workers. It was estimated that the total program would increase from $25 billion to $35 billion.

We may be pressing against the limits of our capacity. Our unit labor costs already exceed most of the world market. Labor leaders understand that problem: we must have the ability to compete. As AFL–CIO president Lane Kirkland recently explained to the Industrial Union Conference: "The nation's manufacturing base must be rebuilt. The American labor movement has a responsibility to develop and pursue adoption of a reindustrialization program, tempered by the experience of the past and the economic realities of the present."

Our gross national product has been shrinking in relative terms. Personal consumption is more popular in America than saving. Fresh investments in new technology will be necessary to restore our competitive position. Perhaps this is not the time to tamper with management's rights to terminate marginal workers.

The Unemployables

For some unfortunate Americans, the problem of termination is irrelevant, because they have a difficult time obtaining any job. When they do find work, they have trouble holding onto it. For many reasons—lack of education, poor work skills, bad attitudes, racial discrimination, poor health, or poverty—some Americans are not employable. They take each new job with the expectation that they will fail, because failure is what they expect of themselves. For such people, being fired seems inevitable. Time after time, they are discharged for cause. By failing to do the job, they insure that they will be fired. The employer has no choice.

These people are the chronic victims of a free society. In America, unemployable people exist in the hundreds of thousands. They drift from job to job like leaves on the sidewalk, blown into heaps by the chill winds of each recession. Impoverished, uneducated, incapable of resisting easy gratification, they circulate from low paid jobs to the state employment office to the streets.

Superimposed on the masses of native-born, marginal workers are wave after wave of immigrants from Mexico, Haiti, and other underdeveloped nations, who come to America looking for work, jobs on any terms, any conditions. Some are handicapped by language or lack of vocational training. They are strangers in an alien culture, struggling to survive in the least attractive precincts of the national job market. These workers can achieve only insecure employment. By and large, they do not become members of unions. They do not have permanent jobs with large organizations. When they are fired, it is done swiftly and without recourse. Nevertheless, they are an important part of the American employment picture. The farmers, the needle trades, and the restaurants of America need them. The American system can be particularly brutal for such people.

As this chapter has discussed, termination can be hard on many workers, even those quite capable of finding and holding a new job. If an employer can take away your job without cause, you have reason to feel insecure. What can you do about it? You can work for the government to be protected by civil service laws. You can join a union. You can ask your new employer for a contract. But are these practical alternatives?

Soon, you may have more protection. The law seems to be changing: termination at will may soon be obsolete. A person who has been fired may believe that termination at will is not a good rule of law. Perhaps employers should be required to take more responsibility for their workers. These ideas are being talked about. Change may be on the horizon.

"When I was fired, I decided that the entire system was totally unfair. I had done my absolute best. Other guys were goofing off. My boss didn't even have the guts to tell me why I had to go. He called me up at home during the weekend and told me not to come in on Monday. That stinks."

The Game Is Changing

IF LARGE NUMBERS OF AMERICAN WORKERS are worried about being fired, they may decide to change the rules. Ira Glasser, executive director of the American Civil Liberties Union, warns that an employee rights movement is "surging across the United States." The chairman of Xerox has stated that employee rights will be a central problem for corporate management for the 1980s. Job security may become a political issue. This chapter will describe some of the changes that already are taking place in the attitudes of employers, in court decisions, and in other countries.

This background is important. When you are about to be involved in a firing, the outcome may depend upon these new trends in legal decisions. What is the law?

Some employers already give their employees more rights than the law requires because they think that job security leads to good morale and better performance. Employment security does not insure that a worker will be productive, loyal to the employer, or trustworthy. Some jobs are boring, dirty, dangerous, or undesirable. Then a sensible person may want to take the money and run! Job security may not matter. But, in most jobs, the worker who is secure may work more productively.

Some successful corporations have come to the conclusion that sound employee relations means being fair to employees. Xerox, for example, has promised its workers that they will not be terminated except for cause. If Xerox is correct in believing that job security is a valuable element in its employment policy, it may be in our national interest to increase the level of security for all American workers.

Changes does seem to be in the air. Professor Alan Westin of Columbia Law School, for one, believes that "powerful political, social and legal changes are at work" demanding expanded employee rights. The April 6, 1981, *Business Week* reported that "The right of employers to fire workers in private industry who are not covered by a union contract . . . is beginning to erode."

Work is a central social issue. Most of us are employees of institutions. We no longer work for ourselves or for individual employers. The language of master and servant no longer seems relevant to the modern workplace. Work in an organization requires relatively uniform and impersonal procedures. We must fit the system. We no longer enjoy personal control over our working days.

The common-law rule that employees can be terminated at will is still central in our employment system, but legislators have already reacted to the demands of powerful interest groups. Some categories of employees have escaped the common-law doctrine. Unions, civil servants, and minority groups each have their own escape hatch. Termination at will remains, stranded, at the center. What now?

To some libertarians, the answer is quite clear: "We must strengthen employee rights. Nothing is more important. Americans must not be totalitarian at the workplace but free on weekends. We are suffering from a split personality." Conservative business executives express a different opinion: "Don't believe that bunk. The American worker gets the best treatment in the history of the world. He is highly productive and well paid. Nobody has better working conditions. Don't screw up a system that is the marvel of the world."

Whom do you listen to? Managers have a vested interest.

Labor leaders have their own axe to grind. Academics may not be realistic. Who speaks for the public?

The Great Termination-at-Will Debate

American society has been changing. In our more secure and socialized era, some people argue that termination at will is obsolete. The traditional theories of contract law upon which the doctrine is based are eroding. Other countries protect workers against arbitrary discharge. Shouldn't we follow suit?

Dean Lawrence E. Blades of the University of Iowa wrote a law-review article in 1967 entitled "Employment at Will vs. Individual Freedom: On Limiting the Abusive Exercise of Employer Power" (67 *Columbia Law Journal* 1404 [1967]). It is often cited by people who think the workers should be protected against being fired. Blades said that the termination-at-will doctrine was inconsistent with modern employee rights. "We have become a nation of employees . . . dependent upon others for our livelihoods." He felt that the law gave too much power to employers. "The philosophy is incompatible with these days of large, impersonal, corporate employers. It does not comport with the need to preserve individual freedom in today's job-oriented, industrial society." Blades believed that the best way to change the system was for courts to provide a remedy for the abusively discharged employee.

According to Blades, the absolute right of discharge gives the employer too much power over employees. This is particularly true, he said, in modern America where the individual worker faces a "narrowing range of alternative employment opportunities as advances in modern technology require more and more specialization." The common-law rule, according to Blades, "forces the nonunion employee to rely on the whim of his employer for the preservation of his livelihood, making him a docile follower of his employer's every wish. . . . It is the fear of being discharged which above all else renders the great majority of employees vulnerable to employer coercion."

Blades particularly felt that the private areas of the employee's life should fall outside such control. He gave examples of "overreaching domination by employers." He cited freedom against self-incrimination, political rights, and right not to be discharged without just cause, as areas most commonly violated by employers. Blades concluded that employee protection was "patently inadequate," particularly for nonunion workers who are psychologically unprepared for the loss of employment. "The fear of discharge, and thus the vulnerability to employer coercion, is especially acute among professional and white-collar employees, the very groups whose numbers are increasing and whose jobs are least likely to be protected by collective bargaining agreements."

Recognizing the significant role of job-security provisions in collective bargaining agreements, Blade said that "the assumption that unions will stand as universal protectors of all employees at every echelon of employment would be an obvious exaggeration." Nor could employees count on individual contracts. Blades pointed out: "Only the unusually valuable employee has sufficient bargaining power to obtain a guarantee that he will be discharged only for just cause."

As a solution to the problem of unjust discharge, Blades favored arming the employee with a damage action, which would deter an employer from discharging an employee for an abusive reason. "The fear of lawsuits would have the salutory effect of discouraging improper attempts to interfere with the employee's personal integrity and freedom. Legal protection for the abusively discharged employee would inevitably develop a keener awareness of and greater respect for the individuality of the employee."

Blades carefully documented the state of the law governing the modern employment relationship. He pointed out that the industrial revolution had destroyed any personal relationship between servant and master but that courts have not recognized this change. He blamed courts reluctance to change upon the obsolete legal theory of "mutuality." "So long as courts are unwilling to liberalize their view, it is unlikely that the employer's right to terminate the at-will employment relationship will be curtailed by contract law." The states should cut through to a solution by devising a new legal remedy.

Blades said that state legislation should protect employees against "interference with the freedom or integrity of the employee in respects which bear no reasonable relationship to the employment or which do not advance the legitimate interest of the employer." The courts should be permitted to define the statute on a case by case basis. He did admit that the prospect of such legislative reform was dim: "There is no strong lobby to protest and promote these ideas."

> Employees having diverse job specialities and working at varying echelons of employment are simply not equipped to form a cohesive group with enough power to influence legislators. The unlikelihood that such legislation will be enacted in the foreseeable future is enhanced by the strong interest groups to be counted on to oppose it. One need not be an extreme cynic to say that employers would not favor such legislation. Nor could organized labor be expected to favor laws which would give individual employees a means of protecting themselves without need of a union. Therefore, it appears that protection of all employees from the abusive exercise of employer power will have the originate, if it is to be established at all, in the courts.

Blades should receive high marks for prophetic wisdom.

Labor unions remain lukewarm, although a few union spokesmen are beginning to talk about just-cause protection for non-union workers. Jules Bernstein, counsel for the Laborers International Union, thinks that the National Labor Relations Board should have the right to hear individual discharge cases. According to him, the single employee is helpless in dealing with an employer. Bernstein admits that employers would be violently opposed to his plan, as they indeed are.

No significant pressure groups have formed to change the law. How can one expect workers who have been fired or laid off to exert significant political pressure? They are already fully engaged with trying to cope with their personal problem of "psychic survival."

Dr. Norward Roussell of the Mott Foundation studied the situation in Flint, Michigan, during the massive auto layoffs of the mid-seventies. He discovered that over half the city's families had been disrupted by unemployment. Thousands of men and women had their lives and egos destroyed by unemployment.

Why don't such communities organize? Why don't they demand that government do something to insure that jobs be made available. A local union president in Flint may have the answer: "They beat up on themselves, literally and figuratively. But they don't raise hell with the union or the company." They don't organize a militant lobby for legislative change. "In fact, when they get called back, they thank G.M."

Unemployed workers become preoccupied by their own problems, traumatized by the numbing experience of having lost their jobs, cut off from the other unemployed people who are going through the same experience. Moreover, a schism often appears between the employed and the unemployed, even between members of the same union. Some more enlightened unions, the UAW for example, provide welfare programs for their unemployed members and have negotiated costly supplementary benefits. In other unions, the terminated employee drops off the list, a forgotten person.

Outside the union sector, people with jobs seem even less concerned with the unemployed. "There, but for the grace of God, go I. But don't talk to me about job sharing."

After Dean Blades' law-review article in 1967, other calls for reform began to appear. At first, the courts did not seem to be listening. They continued to rule that nonunion employees could be discharged "for good cause, for bad cause, or for no cause at all." Nor did labor lawyers seem much concerned about termination at will. The doctrine was seldom discussed. Critics say that a conspiracy of silence maintains termination at will as one of the "dirty secrets" of American labor law.

Termination at will is an artifact from those "good old days" when labor was purchased as a commodity. Times have changed, but the common law accommodates slowly, particularly, when dealing with legal doctrines that provide an economic advantage to powerful interest groups. In our free society, no more powerful interest exists than corporate employers.

Termination at will may be eroding. Some court decisions are expanding the rights of discharged workers. If an employee has given "consideration" at the time of employment, for example, foregoing the right to compete, or if the discharge violates a public policy, or indicates a malicious intent, or impinges upon some protected personal right of the employee, then the case may fall within an exception to the doctrine.

Employee lawsuits based upon such concepts are hard to win. Employees seldom prevail in the absence of a protective statute or an employment contract. Short of going to court, nonunion employees can only complain directly to management.

Some people worry about what would happen if employees were encouraged to file such claims. The present trickle of employee-rights cases in the courts might become a torrent if legislation protecting all workers from unjust dismissal were adopted by the states or by Congress, particularly if awards include punitive damages. Our courts are already swamped with lawsuits, so congested that cases take years to try. This country does not need more litigation. Any extension of employee discharge rights that would dump tens of thousands of lawsuits into the courts would be a disaster. The impact on the national court system might be tragic.

Moreover, the current emphasis in labor relations has been to tone down the adversarial climate. Creating a new cause of action for litigating employee complaints might unleash additional hostility, which could sabotage efforts to increase productivity. By encouraging employee claims, the law might pit worker against employer in a direct and unpleasant way.

"When I lost my job, I felt very bitter. The last thing I needed was to quarrel with management. I never wanted to see those bastards again, much less to see them in court. I do think that they were unfair. But just for my own survival, I have learned to put things behind me. It was a disappointment but, once it happened, I turned to the next problem, getting a new job. That is the healthy way, don't you think?"

Jack Stieber, a professor at Michigan State University, has also championed state legislation to protect nonunion workers against unfair dismissal. "This can be accomplished through legislation which would permit employees, who have completed a period of probationary employment and are not otherwise protected against unfair dismissal, to appeal the discharge penalty to an arbitrator." Stieber favors a system of government arbitrators somewhat like the industrial tribunals found in Great Britain, West Germany, or France.

Stieber estimates that each year in the United States a million nonunion employees are discharged without a fair hearing. This includes executives and clerical personnel as well as blue-collar workers. Union members and public employees would be exempt from Stieber's proposed law since they are already protected by collective bargaining provisions or civil-service laws. Such a law would add another layer of regulation, setting up a new government agency and creating more litigation between employers and their employees.

Another enthusiast for such legislation is Robert G. Howlett, former chairman of the Michigan Employment Relations Commission. He too believes that employees in nonunion enterprises should be protected against being discharged without just cause and that the states could provide "the better forum." Howlett cites Justice Brandeis: "One of the happy incidents of the federal system is that a single courageous state may, if its citizens choose, serve as a laboratory and try novel social and economic experiments without risk to the rest of the country."

Some interest has been expressed in such an approach: in South Carolina, the department of labor is authorized to mediate disputes between employees and their employers over involuntary terminations. In Connecticut, a bill was introduced in the legislature in 1973 to provide "just cause" protection to unorganized workers. Management opposed the legislation. It was defeated. Similar bills are pending in Michigan and New Jersey. Howlett admits that the idea has limited appeal to legislators. "Unorganized employees have no formal groups. Hence, they have little impact on elections."

Even if such a law were likely to pass, difficult technical problems would arise. Should the jurisdiction be limited to discharge? How should "just cause" be determined? Howlett would prefer to place the administration of the act under the state department of labor. Under his scheme, discharge claims would be filed with the agency. A staff mediator would first attempt to resolve the problem. Then, the agency would be authorized to provide a screening process, using an examining magistrate to determine whether the grievance had merit. After that, the case would be ripe for arbitration.

Howlett envisions the use of outside arbitrators paid by the state. The grievant would be represented by "an experienced official of the administrating agency." He points out that "individual employees seldom have the competence necessary to marshall evidence and present it effectively." Such a scheme would involve a major intervention by state government into the employment process. It might pour gasoline on an already inflamed employment relationship, providing a new arena for the squabbles of employees and managers, a radical expansion in employee rights. There is no indication that the American public is calling for such a law.

Laws of the type that Steiber and Howlett are recommending would require new regulatory agencies or expand the duties of existing agencies. New regulations could lead to endless controversy and litigation. Do we need to add another layer of controversy to our already contentious society?

Many recent law-review articles have urged that nonunion employees be protected against unjust discharge. Professor Clyde

Summers of the University of Pennsylvania maintains that this is a matter of "simple justice." He "is appalled by the employers' insistence that the open door provides a fair review." In most cases, there is no adequate investigation of the facts. Management maintains entire control of the process. He says that employers don't want to provide justice: they want "dispute burial."

Summers claims that such a change would be in management's best interest, would be an enlightened human-resource policy. "Guaranteeing individual rights and providing fair procedures to employees is a social obligation of management. The fact that an employee has legal recourse puts pressure on all levels of management to police their procedures, examine their decisions, and correct their mistakes."

In an article in the *Harvard Business Review,* Summers noted that union workers "have a more complete and sensitive security against unjust discipline, more efficient procedures, and more effective remedies than employees in any other country in the world." Nonunion employees in the United States, on the other hand, are "almost alone in having no statutory protection against unjust dismissal without notice and without cause." He acknowledges that such a system would make life "more difficult for those lower-level supervisors who impose ill-considered or arbitrary discipline and also for those upper-level managers who cannot or will not control their subordinates."

Summers bases his argument on the fact that a policy of treating employees fairly will, in the long run, reassure employees that they will receive equity, softening the image of an autocratic management. He praises Lockheed, Trans World Airlines, and Michael Reese Hospital in Chicago as employers who stand behind their promise to provide fair treatment, submitting claims to impartial arbitration. He says that termination at will is based upon defective legal precedents and runs "counter to accepted principles of personnel practices and social values, indeed counter to all recognition of the employee's interest in his position, all sense of fairness, and all principles of due process."

Professor Julius G. Getman of the Yale Law School has also written extensively on the subject. He believes that neither managers nor employees are happy with the present state of the law. "Agitation is growing for some kind of 'good-cause' statutory job protection for all workers." He notes that an increasing number of statues prevent employers from dismissing employees. The National Labor Relations Act prohibits firing workers for union activity. The Equal Employment Opportunity Act and similar laws protect against discharges based on race, sex, national origin, or religion. Veterans and handicapped workers have their own employment umbrellas. People who complain about working conditions are protected by the Occupational Safety and Health Act. Local laws protect workers on the basis of sexual preference or marital status.

Getman notes that managers are sometimes harassed by workers who use the enforcement machinery provided by these various laws. If a discharged person loses in one tribunal, there is nothing to stop a renewed claim in another. "A politically active, elderly, handicapped, black woman might bring charges against a company in four or five different forums under eight or nine different theories. An employer who wins in one forum might lose in the next."

Reports of a running battle between one woman and a major national business publication would seem to bear that out. When she was hired, she was encouraged to believe that she would soon become an executive. She expressed a strong desire to move into management. At first, her performance was praised. Then relationships began to sour. The pressure of the job resulted in various health problems and periods of absence for which she received reprimands. She persuaded her union to file a grievance alleging company harassment. The union discussed the grievance with the company but refused to take the matter to arbitration.

Now she was angry at both organizations. She filed a sex-discrimination complaint against both, claiming that she had been cheated out of sales bonuses. More than a year later, EEOC found that a general pattern of discrimination existed, but that the company had not discriminated personally against the claimant. The grievant was unhappy with the result, claiming that the EEOC did not understand how sales bonuses were established in the publishing business.

The EEOC's determination of a class violation resulted in a conciliation agreement under which the employer agreed to stop discriminating against its female employees. In the company newsletter, the president emphasized his committment to affirmative action. After the EEOC proceeding, the employer's attitude toward the grievant vacillated. At first, some accounts were taken away from her. Later, in an effort to placate her, management attempted to credit the grievant for sales actually made by the sales manager. She would have none of it. She questioned the propriety of such an arrangement. At first, management encouraged her to accept the extra bonus. When she persisted, the offer was withdrawn. The company was embarrassed. The grievant had secretly tape-recorded the discussions.

Following that attempt to resolve the problem, management's attitude became hostile. Other sales personnel stopped talking to the grievant. The grievant decided that she was being ostracized and that management was trying to alienate her from other staff members. She wrote a letter of complaint to the executive vice president. He left on vacation, without answering. Her health became worse. Her sick days increased. She wrote to the president, requesting an emergency meeting. When she called his office several days later, she learned that the executive vice president had been asked to look into the matter. An appointment was made. When she arrived at his office, she was told that he had canceled the meeting. She was referred to her boss, the man she was complaining about. She became ill and left to seek medical attention.

On the following day, she was fired and denied severance pay. She sent a full report of her problems to the company's board of directors. She requested her union to file for arbitration. At the same time, she filed another complaint with the EEOC and applied for benefits under New York State Unemployment. The company defended itself in all three tribunals. A New York State Administrative Law Judge heard the unemployment insurance claim. The hearings became voluminous. The company attempted to prove that she had been discharged for misconduct. The grievant submitted tape-recordings of her conversations with company officials. After three separate hearings, the judge upheld the grievant. "Her conduct did not rise to the level of misconduct. . . . The testimony does not prove insubordination." The company appealed to the Review Board, which affirmed the decision.

Shortly after that victory, she filed another sex-discrimination complaint against the company with the New York City Human Rights Commission. Many months later, her many disputes with the company were finally settled.

This woman's battle with her employer and her union continued for almost five years. It cost the company a vast amount of executive time. It precipitated a class action. It created unpleasant confrontations in several forums. Would a more sympathetic treatment of this woman's problems have resolved the dispute at an earlier stage? Would an internal complaint procedure have avoided the need for so much outside litigation? Would a single labor tribunal be preferable to the present system of multiple forums?

Professor Getman thinks that employers would be eager to change the present system. "In return for accepting the good-cause standard, employers could ask for a limit on the number of agencies that can sit in judgment on management attempts to discipline or fire unsatisfactory employees. All, or nearly all, current restrictions on firing could be incorporated into a simple standard, enforced through a single agency similar to the National Labor Relations Board."

Getman's suggestion may not be feasible. The American political system seems to be based upon single interest advocacy. The agencies established in response to relatively narrow employee protection pressures represent strong vested interests. It seems unlikely that the Getman "compromise" would be accepted.

Court Decisions That Protect Employees
from Being Fired

Other reformers look to the courts for change. In their writings, they encourage judges to adopt doctrines such as "abusive discharge" or "implied contract of employment" which would give certain discharged employees a new cause of action.

State courts seem to be moving in that direction. It is hard to tell whether the trend will continue. In recent years, Congress has been protective of employee rights. During the same period, our economic growth has faltered. If worker rights are further expanded, it may be at the expense of cost efficiency, making it more difficult to strengthen the economy to meet the challenge of world competition.

There seems little doubt that Congress could expand such protection if it wished to do so. In *NLRB v. Jones & Laughlin Steel Corporation,* the Supreme Court upheld the Railway Labor Act's prohibition against firing employees on account of union activity. Since that case, courts have recognized that Congress can protect an employee against being discharged in violation of a specific public policy. Most authorities believe that a law prohibiting unjust dismissal would be upheld by the courts.

Decisions based on the absence of mutuality are of questionable vitality. Judges have shot that doctrine full of holes. Authorities suggest that it should be abandoned. Where an employee has furnished "good consideration," courts have held that the absence of mutuality does not foreclose a finding that the employment was intended to be permanent. The enforceability of "just-cause" provisions in collective bargaining agreements also indicates that the mutuality argument is dying, if not dead.

Another rationale for termination at will was that the worker had not paid anything extra for job security. The employer never promised to continue the employment. This is called "lack of consideration," a legal doctrine that seems quite bizarre. The modern tendency has been to consider the reality of the expectations of individuals involved in a transaction and the social implications that may result from assigning legal burdens.

Some recent cases indicate a change in judicial attitudes. Watching the law develop is like observing the face of a glacier. Nothing seems to be happening; then, with no warning, a huge segment will break away, leaving an entirely new shape.

The New Theory of Abusive Discharge

An employee of Local 396 of the International Brotherhood of Teamsters in California was discharged for refusing to commit perjury when testifying before a legislative investigatory body. The court granted the employee's claim of wrongful discharge. More recently, in *Tameny v. Atlantic Richfield Company,* the California Supreme Court sent a case to trial where a sales representative alleged that he was fired when he refused to "threaten, cajole and pressure" private gas station owners into lowering their pump prices, which would have been a price-fixing violation. The suit had been dismissed by the lower courts for failing to state a cause of action.

The case illustrates an inventive lawyer creating new theories of liability. The employee claimed that he was wrongfully discharged for refusing to participate in the illegal scheme. He had worked for the company for fifteen years. In 1975, he was a retail sales representative dealing with various ARCO service stations in Bakersfield. He was told to persuade his stations to reduce prices. When he refused to do so, he was fired.

His lawyer offered five separate theories: wrongful discharge, breach of implied covenant of good faith and fair dealing, interference with contractual relations, breach of contract, and treble damages under an antitrust statute. This broadside of legal actions is particularly impressive against the fact that the California Labor Law provides that an employment contract having no specific term is terminable at the will of either party.

The plaintiff abandoned his contract claims during the proceedings but persisted in his tort action for wrongful discharge. The Supreme Court of California reviewed various decisions in favor of employees discharged for refusing to commit perjury, union activity, serving on a jury, filing for worker's compensation, or reporting violations of law by the employer. It concluded that discharging an employee for refusing to violate the law was a tort. The court noted that the "days when a servant was practically the slave of his master have long since passed." The case was remanded for trial. Damages may be substantial since, under tort law, they are not limited to compensation. Punitive damages may be awarded.

A strong dissent was filed by Justice Clark. The state statute provided two specific exceptions to termination at will, absence from work to serve as an election officer and participation in labor activities. He criticized the majority for indulging in judicial legislation. Nevertheless, the ARCO case has extended the potential liability of California employers. Recent cases involving American Airlines and See's Candy, Inc. in San Francisco have given liberal protection to long service employees.

Some state courts have upheld employees who were fired for filing unemployment insurance claims; others have not. In general, an employee cannot be fired for refusing to commit a crime or to violate a public law. Courts in Pennsylvania and Oregon have held that damages can be awarded where an employee is fired for serving on a jury against the wishes of the employer. A West Virginia court held in favor of an officer of a bank who was fired for telling the authorities that the bank had overcharged customers.

It is difficult to forecast what a particular court will decide. In a recent case in Colorado, a head nurse was fired for failing to comply with an order to reduce her staff in the intensive care unit in the hospital. She claimed that she was obliged to maintain safe conditions because she was a licensed professional nurse. The court held that the state licensing code for nurses merely prescribed a general standard of conduct and would not support a wrongful discharge action.

In 1979, a New Jersey court held that a physician who had been fired by the Ortho Pharmaceutical Corporation for refusing to test children with a drug with a high saccharin content should be given an opportunity to show that her discharge was unlawful because it had a "substantial impact on matters of public interest, including health and safety." The court expressed reluctance to tamper with the termination-at-will doctrine. "A public policy exception would represent a departure from the well-settled, common-law, employment-at-will rule. If such a departure is to be made, care is required in order to insure that the reasons underlying the rule will not be undermined. Most notably in this regard, the employer's legitimate interest in conducting his business and employing and retaining the best personnel available cannot be unjustifiably impaired. Thus, it cannot change the present rule which holds that just or good cause for the discharge of an employee at will or the giving of reasons therefore is not required. In addition, the exception must guard against a potential flood of unwarranted disputes and litigation that might result. . . ." Ultimately, the doctor was unable to demonstrate that her case came under the exception.

Such cases are based on the recognized exception to the doctrine, a strong public policy. Could an exception also be created, based solely on the personal rights of the employee? We are back staring at the face of glacier. Judicial opinions whisper that a new doctrine is about to be born. Then a major court decision restructures the entire system. A segment of obsolete law collapses and is replaced by more modern doctrines. Is that about to happen in the law of employee rights?

A 1974 case from New Hampshire is frequently cited to demonstrate the judiciary's willingness to change the present law. Before coming to the United States, Olga Monge worked as a schoolteacher in Costa Rica. In order to obtain a teaching certificate in New Hampshire, she needed a degree from an American college. In 1968 she took a job with Beebe Rubber Company as a machine operator for $1.84 an hour. She worked the night shift, using her earnings to pay her college expenses. After working without incident for three months, she bid for an opening on a press at higher wages. Her foreman told her that if she wanted the job, she would have to be "nice" to him. When she got the job, at $2.79 an hour, her foreman asked her for a date. She refused, being married, with three children. After working on the press for several weeks, she was assigned to another job at $1.99 an hour. Her overtime was taken away. When she asked her foreman about these changes, he told her that she could sweep floors and clean bathrooms if she needed extra money.

She began to receive annoying phone calls at her home. She complained to the plant's personnel manager, but to no avail. He knew that the foreman used his position to force himself upon female employees. She was told "not to make trouble." After another argument with the foreman, she became ill and was hospitalized for several weeks. She called in each day to say that she would not be in. After a few days the personnel manager marked her down as a "voluntary quit," and hired someone to fill her job.

The Supreme Court of New Hampshire ruled that "the foreman's overtures and the capricious firing . . . the seeming manipulation of job assignments, and the apparent connivance of the personnel manager support the jury's conclusion that the dismissal was maliciously motivated." It remanded the case to the lower court for a determination of damages.

The court recognized that "in all employment contracts, whether at will or for a definite term, the employer's interest in running his business as he sees fit must be balanced against the interest of the employee in maintaining his employment, and the public's interest in maintaining a proper balance between the two. We hold that a termination by the employer of a contract of employment at will which is motivated by bad faith or malice or based on retaliation is not the best interest of the economic system or the public good and constitutes a breach of the employment contract."

Justice Grimes disagreed: the plaintiff's "final termination was in accordance with established company rules. . . . A finding that this company discharged the plaintiff because she refused to date her foreman eight months before could not reasonably be made." He noted that the foreman had disputed the plaintiff's allegations. Since Olga Monge was a member of the union, she was protected by the "just-cause" provisions of the contract and could not be terminated at will. Justice Grimes went on, "Not a single case has been found which supports the broad rule laid down by the court. . . . The law everywhere, uniformly supported by scores of cases is that an employment contract for an indefinite period is one at will and is terminable at any time by either party regardless of motive for 'good cause, bad cause or no cause' and for 'any reason or no reason.'"

Since the Monge case, many state courts have continued to uphold employee terminations, even in situations that seem unfair. In Arizona, the Court of Appeals upheld the dismissal of two employees for refusing to take a voice-stress, lie-detector test at the request of the company. Illinois confirmed the dismissal of a man who was fired for complaining about his supervisor. A court in Kentucky dismissed a claim by an employee who was fired after he announced that he would be going to law school at night.

On the other hand, a few trial courts have begun to cite the Monge case with approval. In *Savodnik v. Korvettes* in the Federal District Court in Brooklyn, New York, Judge Thomas C. Platt recently held that an employee who claimed to have been fired because his pension was about to vest could obtain a trial; he described the cause of action as one of abusive discharge.

The New Theory of Implied Contract

In *Voorhees v. Shriners Hospital for Crippled Children,* a 1980 case, the Superior Court of the State of Washington created a theory of liability based upon the employer's own personnel policies.

Juanita Voorhees had been working at the hospital as a registered nurse for six years. One evening, she playfully tossed a few drops of water at a patient, a healthy, cheerful young man with his leg in a cast. In his turn, he threw a paper cup of water at her. She immediately wiped up the water from the floor. Later on, he again threw some water at her: she threw some back. Again, she wiped up the water. Everyone had a good laugh.

Unfortunately, Voorhees' supervisor didn't see any humor in the incident. The supervisor filed a report, and in due course Voorhees was fired for "gross violation or neglect of job responsibility, which endangers the welfare of a patient" and for "physical abuse of patients." Nurses at Shriners were not members of a union.

Nurse Voorhees took the hospital to court, claiming that the hospital did not have a good reason for discharging her. The judge studied the hospital's printed personnel policies, which specified that they were not intended to be a written employment contract. The hospital claimed that it could terminate nurses at will.

Nurse Voorhees, presenting a novel theory of contract law, pointed out that the booklet said that "during the probationary period" an employee could be discontinued without notice. Afterward, employees became "permanent." Other employees testified that they understood that they could be terminated only for cause.

Based on the booklet and the testimony of witnesses, the court concluded that there was "an implied agreement that a permanent employee is terminable only for just cause." The judge decided that Nurse Voorhees' conduct did not justify discharge. He awarded her damages.

If accepted by other courts as an appropriate rule, this case could have a broad impact. Many personnel policies of nonunion employers provide for a "trial period" before the employee becomes a "regular" or "permanent" employee. For example, the American Arbitration Association's own employee booklet puts it this way:

> The first three months of employment with the AAA are considered a trial period—both for you and for the Association. During this period, you will be learning about

your job and how it fits into the total picture of Association activities. During this time we will learn how well you can perform assigned tasks. After completing this "getting acquainted" period, you will be eligible to participate in the benefits of employment described in this booklet.

If courts interpret such a provision as an implied agreement that after the trial period an employee becomes permanent and can only be terminated for just cause, employers will be careful what they print in employee manuals. Until recently, these booklets were not viewed as contracts. Employers usually accentuate the benefits of employment. Little thought has been given to protective language. Now some employers may protect themselves by including a statement that they have the right to discharge any employee with or without cause. Others may stop publishing such booklets or hand the entire problem over to their lawyers.

Two decisions from the Supreme Court of Michigan in 1980 also extended employer liability on the basis of implied contract. Both claims concerned executives who were fired, allegedly without just cause. Charles Toussaint, who was terminated by Blue Cross/Blue Shield of Michigan, based his claim on a provision in a supervisory manual which said that it was the "policy" of the company to terminate employees "for just cause only." Executive Walter Ebling, fired by Masco Corporation, claimed that before taking the position he was assured that "he would not be discharged if he was doing his job."

The court held that job security could be established by express agreement, oral or written, or as a result of the employee's legitimate expectations based upon the employer's statements. In both cases, the court held that even where employment is for an indefinite term, a promise by the employer to terminate only for cause, made orally or in an employee manual, may create an enforceable right.

Where an employer chooses to establish such policies and practices and makes them known to its employees, the employment relationship is presumably enhanced. The employer secures an orderly, cooperative and loyal work force, and the employee the peace of mind associated with job security and the conviction that he will be treated fairly.

If an employer promises, in writing or by oral assurances, that the employee will be terminated only for cause, a legal obligation may be created. The court said, "We conclude that the question whether termination was for cause was for the jury." A jury may be asked to decide whether an employee was discharged for unsatisfactory work.

Corporations will not enjoy having juries review their discharge decisions. As the Michigan court pointed out, "There is the danger that [the jury] will substitute its judgment for the employer's. If the jurors would not have fired the employee for doing what he admittedly did, the employer may be held liable for damages."

If employers do not want such issues to be decided by a jury, they must provide an alternative. The court emphasized that point. "The employer can avoid the perils of jury assessment by providing for an alternative method of dispute resolution. A written agreement could, for example, provide for binding arbitration on the issues of cause and damages."

The importance of these Michigan decisions is to raise the possibility that employers will be forced to make good on their promises. Often, in job interviews, an applicant will ask whether the position is secure. If the employer says not to worry, that employees are terminated only for cause, or if he brags that no employee is discharged unfairly, the basis of a claim may exist. If such a case goes to an average American jury, the employee's likelihood of success may be excellent. Toussaint was awarded $72,000 against Blue Cross/Blue Shield. Ebling got $300,000.

When the Washington and Michigan decisions are brought to the attention of personnel directors, how will they react? Will companies warn employees that they can be terminated at the sole discretion of management? Will they tell their managers not to promise job security? Or will they continue to believe that they are quite free to discharge workers?

At the least, we should see a renewed interest in the language of employee manuals. In the past, these documents have been used to convince employees that the company is a friendly place to work, with generous benefit packages. Now lawyers will read them more carefully, calculating the employer's exact legal exposure. Would a fair reading of the document give an employee the impression that he will be terminated only for cause? If so, a jury might find that the employer is liable for damages.

Justice is like a coral reef. It is built on the dead aspirations of insignificant people who leave the bones of their cases as stepping stones for future generations. One woman is upset because she is demoted for refusing to date her foreman. Another becomes a gadfly because she is denied the executive training that she has been promised. A Hispanic worker resents having to speak English to his co-workers. Each one adds something to the common law of worker's rights. Are they building a promised land? A reef? Or is each case a new barnacle on the ship of state? Take your pick.

In the 1977 case of *Fortune v. National Cash Register Company,* the Supreme Judicial Court of Massachusetts added to the mosaic. Orville E. Fortune had been employed under a written "salesman's contract," terminable by either party upon written notice. Fortune received a weekly salary, plus a bonus for sales made within his "territory," whether the sale was made by him or someone else. The amount was to be determined on the basis of credits, computed on the price of the product sold.

Fortune's territory included First National. He had obtained several orders from that company, including a million-dollar order in 1963. When NCR introduced a new cash register, Fortune tried to interest First National. He helped to arrange a demonstration. Other NCR people were also working on the account.

Soon thereafter, Fortune found a notice on his desk. He was terminated, but asked to "stay on" to smooth out the necessary details. He remained on the job. Later, he received partial bonus commissions on the First National order. After receiving 75 percent of the bonus, Fortune asked for the balance. He was told to "forget about it."

Approximately eighteen months after receiving his "termination" notice, Fortune was asked to retire. He was sixty-one years old, with a son in college. When he refused, he was fired. He sued NCR for the balance of his bonus payments. The court found for Fortune:

> The contract at issue is a classic terminable at will employment contract. It is clear that the contract itself reserved to the parties an explicit power to terminate the contract without cause on written notice. It is also clear that under the express terms of the contract Fortune has received all the bonus commissions to which he is entitled. Thus, NCR claims that it did not breach the contract, and that it has not further liability to Fortune. According to a literal reading of the contract, NCR is correct. . . . We hold that NCR's written contract contains an implied covenant of good faith and fair dealing, and a termination not made in good faith constitutes a breach of contract. . . . Good faith and fair dealing are pervasive requirements in our law: it can be said fairly, that parties to contracts or commercial transactions are bound by this standard.

The court discussed the earlier Monge case in its opinion:

> We believe that the holding in the Monge case merely extends to employment contracts the rule that in *every* contract there is an implied covenant that neither party shall do anything which will have the effect of destroying or injuring the right of the other party to receive the fruits of the contract, which means that in *every* contract there exists an implied covenant of good faith and fair dealing. In the instant case, we need not pronounce our adherence to so broad a policy, nor need we speculate as to whether the good faith requirement is implicity in every contract for employment at will.

Fortune had a right to be compensated for the work that he had done under his employment contract.

Special Legislation for Sales Reps

There are about 800,000 sales representatives in the United States. They are not employees. They invest their own time and re-sources to develop an assigned sales territory. They are indepen-dent contractors who are compensated on a commission basis and who pay their own expenses; they are not covered under unem-ployment insurance or other benefit programs. They are subject to termination or reduction in their territories or product lines.

Recently, a Sales Representative Protection Act was intro-duced by Congressman Ottinger of New York. It would require that sales contracts include a fair provision for termination. The contract may provide for arbitration of disputes, including whether the termination was for "good cause." That term is de-fined as conduct which constitutes dishonesty, fraud or other il-legal activity, a breach of the contract, failure to put forth a good-faith effort, or gross negligence.

The parallel between sales representatives working on a con-tract basis and salesmen working for commissions is quite strik-ing. If sales reps are to be protected against being terminated, it seems unfair that salesmen who bind themselves exclusively to one business firm should not be protected in some way.

First Amendment Cases

When First Amendment rights are involved, it is already pos-sible for a discharged employee to have a day in court. Two mail handlers at the bulk mail center in Sharonville, Ohio, came to work wearing buttons saying "Death to the Shah—get your bloody hand off Iran." Their co-workers threatened to beat them up. At first, the supervisor acted with admirable restraint, warning other workers that they would be disciplined if violence took place. On the following day, the two workers added anti-Shah T-shirts to their repetoire. The supervisor lost his patience. When they refused to remove the buttons and the T-shirts, he fired them for refusing to obey a direct order.

The workers went to court, demanding to be put back to work. Judge Donald S. Porter decided that the Postal Service had to respect free speech. Putting these employees back on the job might cause some minor inconvenience, but their constitutional rights were paramount. A government agency cannot fire a worker for saying something that makes other people angry. Employees of the Postal Service are covered by the First Amendment.

In another case involving the Constitution, an employee claimed that his religious rights were being violated. In addition to serving as a Methodist minister, he had been employed in a warehouse in Pike County, Georgia, for nine years. When he could be spared, the company allowed him to perform his pastoral duties. During 1971, five such absences were approved. On one occasion, the supervisor denied a request. When the grievant did not come to work, he was suspended without pay and warned that if he did it again, he would be fired. Several months later, he asked to be excused on a Saturday to officiate at a funeral. The supervisor again told him that he couldn't be spared because a sale was being held at the company's store. The minister failed to come to work. He was fired. A district court upheld the discharge, finding that his absence caused "undue hardship."

On appeal, the decision was confirmed: "There is substantial evidence showing genuine business need for the plaintiff's presence on the day in question and the disruption caused by his absence." The "day in question" was in 1971. The decision of the Court of Appeals was issued on April 7, 1980. It took nine years for the federal courts to decide a question that could have been determined by an arbitrator in a few months. How many warehouse workers have the fortitude to persevere for so many years?

Public employees who view their employment as a lifetime

career and can take advantage of available civil-service remedies may be more likely to embark upon a safari through the courts. Many employee-rights frontiers have been explored by government workers. Even where First Amendment rights are not involved, courts have held that due-process protections are available in public employment. The absence of a contract does not preclude such protection. Courts in several states have upheld such claims, based upon the employer's failure to demonstrate just cause for termination.

Laying aside legal theories, many people believe that the present American rule is unfair. An employee who has worked for many years with one employer may be discharged without justification. When that happens, the system seems cruel and threatening, so that the other employees work in fear of being fired. That is not right, they say. Reasonable job security should be extended to every worker, as long as there is work to be done and the employee is willing and able to do the job.

Employees covered by collective bargaining agreements or civil-service provisions have job security. Other private employees have no such protection. Why shouldn't every employee be treated the same?

The Whistle Blower

Often, employees are the only people to know that a law is being violated or that their employer's product is defective. It can be argued that there is a public interest in encouraging them to "blow the whistle."

An engineer believes that a product is dangerous and that his warnings within the organization are being ignored. Should he be encouraged to publicize the situation to protect the public interest? Many businessmen think that this is a dangerous idea. A professional employee may be mistaken. The engineer may be wrong or may have ulterior motives. In any case, what about loyalty to the employer? The public benefit in encouraging or permitting whistle blowing must be weighed against the problem that it presents to the responsible employer.

These are not rhetorical questions. Technology has gained immense powers, both for benefiting people and for poisoning the environment. Increasing numbers of professionals find themselves in uncomfortable dilemmas, torn between conflicting interests. Finally, the professional societies have become concerned.

Some twenty engineering and scientific societies have issued employment guidelines recognizing their members' obligation to the public by encouraging them to act with "due regard for the safety, life and health of the public and fellow employees." More recently, the American Association for the Advancement of Science went further.

> The protection of individuals from arbitrary action by authority is deeply ingrained in English common law. . . . We believe that some form of due process should be an essential part of any employer–employees agreement or contract, to protect the employee from arbitrary action by the employer, allegedly based on professional or personal misconduct . . . codes of professional ethics are likely to be ineffective unless some type of due process is provided for the resolution of disputes. Without this scientific freedom is likely to be abridged. We therefore strongly recommend that all employment contracts involving scientific or professional employment include such provisions for the review of disputes through hearing and appeal processes. Provision for neutral or third-party participation is important, particularly where issues of public interest are involved.

The AAAS report described a situation involving the BART rapid transit system in San Francisco, whose automated control system had been touted as an innovation in mass transit. Several engineers working on the project became concerned about its safety. Their internal warnings were ignored. They took their concerns to a member of the BART Board of Directors. A public hearing was held, following which the board supported management. The three engineers were given the classic option, resign or be fired. They chose to be fired.

Subsequently, the control system failed on several occasions, causing injuries to passengers. The trains had to be controlled manually. When the California Society of Professional Engineers investigated the matter, it concluded that the three engineers had acted in the best interest of the public. A lawsuit was filed by the engineers.

New protection has been provided to whistle blowers by recent public interest laws. For example, the U.S. Labor Department is required to protect a worker who is fired for publicizing an employer's violation of the Safe Drinking Water Act, the Water Pollution Control Act, the Solid Waste Disposal Act, or the Clean Air Act. "No employee may be discriminated against for trying to uphold the purposes of the act."

A "whistle-blower" who has been threatened or discharged may file a complaint. The agency administering the program must investigate the case to determine whether a violation has occurred. The employer can be ordered to abate the violation and to reinstate the complainant with back pay. Compensatory damages can also be awarded.

In the first two cases testing the law, the employees lost on procedural grounds. In one, a chemist was fired for telling a family that their drinking water might be polluted. The claim was denied because he failed to file within the thirty-day time limit. In another, a radiologist told a patient about a safety violation that had occurred. His job was abolished for "budgetary reasons." With timid enforcement by the Labor Department, these laws may not result in very many victories by employees.

Academic Freedom

The American Association of University Professors has discovered a similar dilemma in recent years. It never wanted to be an advocacy organization, but it became concerned about its members being fired for espousing unpopular views. What to do?

A primary AAUP professional objective has been to protect academic freedom. When a professor is fired for unpopular political beliefs or for being a "troublemaker," AAUP lumbers to the defense by appointing an academic committee to investigate the matter, and to decide whether AAUP should place the university on its censure list.

Recent cases have involved faculty members at Philander Smith College in Arkansas who were fired after they supported certain students who were boycotting classes to protest the condition of campus facilities; an assistant professor at Nichols College in Massachusetts, terminated after he complained about being denied tenure; and a college instructor who was dumped in the middle of the semester because the dean decided that he wasn't a good teacher.

The AAUP tries to protect the professional careers of college teachers against arbitrary decisions by administrators, and it is prepared to investigate violations. It believes that questions of professional competence should be determined by faculty committees, not by the administrative staff.

Administrators will not abdicate their power. They are under pressure to terminate faculty members who are not productive. Many private universities are short of money. Administrators cannot have much patience for unpopular or outmoded teachers. In such a climate, one wonders whether AAUP investigation and censure will accomplish their goals. Perhaps a more direct and effective review procedure would be better.

In recent years, the faculties in some universities have turned toward collective bargaining, reflecting concern about job security. At Yeshiva University in New York City, the faculty became organized shortly after the university closed its Graduate School of Science in 1977 and eliminated certain jobs without advance notice to the faculty. The vote for a union was overwhelming, but the university refused to bargain, claiming that the faculty members were part of management.

The United States Supreme Court, in a controversial 5 to 4 decision, held that the Yeshiva faculty was part of management since faculty committees were involved in hiring and firing, granting tenure and promotions, and establishing curriculum, grades, and academic standards. If faculty members are unable to bargain collectively, union-style grievance arbitration is out of reach. Other options are available. Several universities have installed due-process mechanisms that provide impartial review of personnel decisions affecting faculty members.

A Ford Foundation project called the Center for Mediation in Higher Education is developing model grievance procedures for faculty members. Faculty relations in the universities will be unsettled until the legal issues raised by the Yeshiva case have been resolved. In the meantime, there should be a continuing search for better ways to handle faculty terminations.

Jane McCarthy, who directs the Center, claims that universities are particularly prone to litigation in the courts because their present arrangements for resolving controversies, when coupled with the leisurely academic pace, often lead to an impasse. Investigations, committee reports, and faculty resolutions may be less appropriate techniques for resolving a personnel dispute than a diligent mediator working directly with the administration and the individual involved.

Protection for the Endangered Worker

The Occupational Safety and Health Act protects workers who refuse to carry out dangerous assignments. In *Whirlpool v. Marshall,* two maintenance workers refused to walk on wire mesh, installed twenty feet over the factory floor to catch debris falling from a conveyor belt. When they were asked to climb up on the net, they refused. Earlier, several people had fallen through the screen. One had been killed. The workers were sent home and fined $25.00. After they complained to the Labor Department, a lawsuit found its way to the U.S. Supreme Court. Their right to refuse was upheld.

As Justice Potter Stewart wrote for the majority, "The Act does not wait for an employee to die or become injured." The regulation gives a worker the right to refuse to do a job when "a reasonable person would conclude that there is a real danger of death or serious injury and there is insufficient time, due to the urgency of the situation, to eliminate the danger through resort to statutory enforcement channels." For example, a worker who is fired for refusing to cut metal near an open gas tank, might be reinstated. Through OSHA and similar laws, government has intervened in the employment relationship. Worker rights have been strengthened by such legislation.

Civil-Rights Protection

Equal Employment laws protect many categories of employees and has given new vitality to worker rights. The government is obligated to investigate the reasons for dismissal to see whether they violate the law. The Civil Rights Act of 1964 created a major inhibition upon the firing of workers. Personnel directors report that an increasing number of terminations are being contested. Handling these claims is frustrating, complicated, and time consuming. It has been the fastest growing area of employment relations law.

The legislative prohibition against racial discrimination can be far reaching. A bus company fired a driver for growing a beard, on the theory that its customers preferred clean-shaven personnel. The no-beard policy was called good public relations. No, said a federal court. The black employee who had been fired was subject to a skin condition called pseudo folliculitis barbae, a common problem with black males whose hair follicles curve back into their skin after a shave, causing inflamation. The employee had been advised to grow a beard by his doctor. The no-beard rule discriminated against black males. The employee was returned to work with back pay.

The sensitivity of employers to individual charges of discrimination will become more acute since the Supreme Court has authorized the Equal Employment Opportunity Commission to file class-action suits without having to get the approval of a federal judge. Eleanor Holmes Norton, the feisty former EEOC Chair, was delighted with that decision, "It strengthens our power. EEOC must be treated as a prosecutor vindicating the public interest."

The traditional congressional approach has been to protect special interest groups that demand protection. We have laws for employees who are minorities, female, older workers, union members, and civil servants. We provide special protection around policy problems such as pensions or safety on the job. Our legislative process is "turned on" by political pressure. If discharged nonunion workers could develop sufficient pressure, the legislature would probably respond.

Since the massive reforms of the New Deal, when social security, unemployment insurance, and workmens' compensation were created, there have been no major, broad-based reforms of the employment system. To protect all workers against unjust dismissal would be such a change. But at the present time, I do not foresee the passage of such a law.

Legislation by the Courts

If state courts continue the current trend encouraging discharged employees to sue for wrongful discharge, a new surge of litigation may be emerging. Employee discharge cases may proliferate. There seems to be a trend in that direction.

The recent Connecticut Supreme Court case of *Sheets v. Teddy's Frosted Foods* decided that a quality-control director who claimed to have been fired for reporting substandard products to his boss should have the right to prove his case, based upon the public interest in consumer protection. Can any employee who says that he was discharged for protecting the public collect damages from his boss?

Earlier cases turned on a more explicit theory: an employee could not be fired for refusing to break the law, to drive an unlicensed vehicle, or to commit perjury. The public policy need not be expressed in a criminal statute; it may be reflected in a policy against sexual harassment, bad food, or environmental violations. Will the next innovation by the courts involve a general prohibition against unjust termination?

A Groundswell for Reform?

Nonunion workers have not been lobbying for protection. Even plant closings have not created a broad-based movement. Employers continue to lay off thousands of workers. There has been no indication of public revulsion. Most Americans seem to take such events in stride. Only recently have labor unions directed their full attention to the problem of plant closings.

Where termination happens one worker at a time, even less public concern has been expressed. Most individuals accept their termination and apply for unemployment benefits. Legal actions by discharged employees are relatively rare. Their former associates are happy to continue working, relieved that management also did not take their jobs. When someone is discharged, the other workers go about their duties.

Workers who have been fired are often angry. But they don't engage in political action or attempt to change the system. They may rant and rave. They may castigate the employer. They may file a discrimination claim. Usually, they just go home and lick their wounds. They file for unemployment benefits and start looking for another job.

Younger workers may be more demanding. It is said that they

are a new breed. They want to be listened to. Justice and human dignity may be a more vital part of their vision of working life. Some refuse to make their personal lives secondary to their jobs. If they want to go hunting or wear a beard, they expect to be able to do it. They are free spirits, or so they say. They expect their job to be satisfying and worthy of their time. They are frequently dissatisfied even though their compensation and fringe benefits may be better than ever, and their hours shorter.

Their refusal to subordinate themselves to their job does not necessarily diminish their desire for job security. A liberated life style does not mean that a firing will be any less traumatic. They reject work rules that treat people as objects. They demand that they be given a fair shake. They want to be treated with dignity on the job. They say that they are people, not machines. But they may be just as shocked when the boss decides to discard them.

Here they come directly in conflict with traditional concepts of managerial efficiency. On the one hand, younger workers stress the importance of their personal lives: "It may be the owner's money, but it's my life," as one young professional told me. They may be less respectful and obedient than earlier generations. At the same time, they seem to believe that they should have job security for investing their careers in a firm. Their job is something like property, something that should not be taken away without adequate compensation. They argue that job security will bind them to the economic success of the enterprise.

As Jerome M. Rosow of the Work in America Institute puts it, "Better educated, with even higher expectations for their careers, they want more faster." Some employers have tried to satisfy them by installing formal grievance procedures.

Internal Systems for Employee Grievances

More and more corporations are installing internal procedures for handling grievances. According to Professor Alan Westin of

Columbia Law School, only a small percentage of American companies are doing anything special about employee rights. But those companies are being copied by others.

For example, a major New York bank gives its employees a booklet: "Seven Ways to Solve a Problem." It describes the bank's methods for resolving employee complaints. Employees are told to see their supervisor first. "Experience shows most work-related problems really can be solved between the two of you." If the problem is too personal or the employee thinks that discussing it with the supervisor will make it worse, other avenues are available. The employee is urged to make a "private appointment to confidentially discuss" concerns with the personnel department. That department promises to work with the employee and the supervisor to help develop a solution to any personal problem. There is also a counseling unit, for the employee who doesn't want to talk to a supervisor or where discrimination may be involved.

A problem review procedure is also available. "The goal is to reach an equitable solution—one that's fair to all concerned." The procedure has four steps, similar to the grievance procedures in union contracts. The supervisor writes down the facts involved in the "problem." The employee agrees with the description of the issue. The document is then sent to the next level of supervision, which must respond in seven days. The employee has the right to buck the problem to the division head, who must investigate the matter. That review must be completed in seven days. If the employee is not satisfied, a review board can be requested. A vice president of staff relations chairs the board. Four other members are selected at random from a computer list of those staff members who are willing to serve. One of the members will be a vice president; the others are of the same or a higher level than the employee. Within ten days, the review board must make recommendations to the executive in charge of the group. The final decision is made by a high official in the bank.

The bank also maintains a question box so that the employee can remain anonymous. There is a staff advisory service to counsel with the employee on personal or financial problems and to put an employee in touch with appropriate government agencies or private resources, such as a child-care center, a nursing home or an attorney. An appointment can be made with that office at any time. Consultation is also available on a "hot line." The bank's medical department is available for medical problems, including alcoholism and drugs. Again, the help is provided on a confidential basis.

The bank's system has been designed to deal with the various human problems that may worry employees. Such an approach, if administered with concern and sensitivity, will resolve many of the individual grievances that might otherwise fester within the working environment.

The bank does not promise lifetime job security. It does offer a "climate and resources that will enable all staff members to advance on merit as far as their talents and skills will take them. . . ." It promises "pay and benefits that are fair and competitive." It assured its staff that "ideas, concerns and problems are identified and that two-way communication is effectively maintained." It tries to "provide an environment that identifies, encourages, and rewards excellence and innovation." It notes that "respect for human dignity is fundamental to our success."

It does *not* promise that employees will only be discharged for "just cause." The employees of that bank can be terminated at will. The decision of the boss will be "final," as the booklet says.

According to the Conference Board study of 778 companies, two-thrids of the firms without unions have established formal systems through which employees can obtain a hearing to attempt to resolve grievances. These programs tend to be found in larger firms, mainly in manufacturing and finance. They are used by production and clerical workers. Executives and professionals prefer to negotiate directly with management.

Most of the complaints handled by such procedures are questions about the employee's ability to perform the job, working conditions or equipment, the benefit program or wages, personality conflicts with a supervisor or co-workers, sexual harassment, or illegal discrimination. Internal grievance procedures are not designed exclusively to review terminations, but they can be used for that purpose.

Does a Good Grievance Procedure Eliminate the Need for a Union?

As one experienced industrial relations director told me, "The best way to avoid having a union is to act as if you had one." Employers realize that defending the worker's job is a major union service. Union members are protected by just cause and grievance arbitration provisions. A union will file a grievance whenever a member is fired without just cause.

Some nonunion employers have installed internal arbitration systems for unresolved grievances. *Business Week* has called this the "antiunion grievance ploy" thinking that giving the worker a formal grievance procedure helps to beat union organizing campaigns.

According to the Conference Board's survey of corporate grievance procedures, employers create formal grievance procedures to reduce the employees' need for union representation. A partner in a leading Pittsburgh management law firm has said that an effective grievance procedure is "probably the single most important way to keep a union out of a plant."

If employers embark upon a formal grievance procedure in order to avoid having a union, they may be disappointed. If they install a procedure that promises a fair hearing but which fails to deliver, they actually may drive their employees into the hands of a union.

Workers may not have faith in the internal grievance system, and may not use it. Where the program is broadly used, it may still lead to unionization if the employer is not fair with each grievant. The workers may accept the procedures, but demand professional representation.

That happened in the steel industry during the Depression. Some of the large companies established "employee representation plans" which encouraged workers to select other employees to represent them at the company's grievance procedures. The union used those same people to organize the workers. Within a few years, the industry was organized.

Many things have changed. In the 1980's, it may not be so easy to organize an employer who is providing a fair, nonunion grievance procedure. For one reason or another, many employers are installing employee complaint procedures. Personnel departments are being asked to design fair procedures. A variety of techniques is being used. Some companies attempt to mediate the individual problems of their employees, using ombudsmen, conciliators, human resource specialists, and similar techniques. Others rely upon the open door.

Some of these procedures are used to determine whether a worker should have been terminated, to test the fairness of a decision by a first-line supervisor. They enhance job security in the workplace.

If companies decide to go one step further, supplementing their open-door policy with an informal arbitration system, they can easily do so. Such procedures have already been devised by several companies, using the administrative services of the American Arbitration Association. Impartial arbitrators can be appointed directly by the AAA. Arbitrators are experienced in personnel relations and familiar with the arbitration process.

Grievance arbitration systems under collective bargaining contracts have become well accepted for resolving employee disputes, including whether there was just cause for a discharge. That approach can be applied to the nonunion sector of the work force. But there are problems. The situation facing an individual employee is different than when an employee is represented by a union.

As we have seen, the union provides representation to its members from the beginning. At the initial termination interview, most contracts require that the shop steward be present when the individual is being disciplined. If the employer persists in taking action against the grievant, the case may be discussed again and again in the various steps of the grievance procedure. The union represents the grievant at every step. It has an opportunity to provide eloquent and forceful advocacy on behalf of its members.

When the case does go before an arbitrator, the union will know everything about the situation. It will have investigated the action taken by the employer and should know what the employer's witnesses will say at the hearing. The grievant will be represented by an experienced union official or lawyer who had handled many cases in the past and is familiar with arbitration and with the management adversaries.

Contrast that with the position of an individual worker not represented by a union. After being discharged, the grievant will be off company premises. It will not be easy to investigate the facts of the case. If he does discuss his case with higher-level executives, he will not do so from a position of equality. He is an outsider. He may have difficulty obtaining witnesses to testify on his behalf. Other employees will realize that he is a stranger to the working community.

He will be inexperienced at presenting grievances. The arbitration process will be foreign to him. He may need professional representation. The employer may or may not permit him to use an attorney. Many employees can not afford to retain an attorney. The grievant, being out of a job, is likely to be short of money. Even if the arbitrator is authorized to award a sum of money, it may not amount to enough to justify a contingency fee.

Would an arbitrator reinstate the worker? How practical is it to put an employee back to work? In the absence of a union, the supervisor may harass such a worker until he quits. The situation is not the same for a union member who will be protected by the union after being returned to the job.

In a nonunion arbitration system it may be more sensible to restrict the arbitrator to awarding reasonable compensation. The arbitrator might give the employee supplementary payments in addition to unemployment insurance compensation.

There are other technical problems in designing a nonunion arbitration system. But employers can resolve such problems with practical, innovative solutions. At the hearing itself, the individual grievant and the employer should be able to participate in a position of parity. It would not be fair for the employee to have to represent himself, while the employer is represented by the company attorney or a highly trained professional from the personnel department. Some nounion arbitration systems have tried to balance the scale by providing that the personnel department will help the grievant to prepare and present the case, while the supervisor is expected to represent the interests of the company.

A Recommended Grievance Procedure with Arbitration

Based upon my experience with the American Arbitration Association, I would recommend the following grievance procedure for employers who wish to offer arbitration to their nonunion employees.

Initial complaints would be handled in the usual way. The employee would discuss the problem with the immediate supervisor. The supervisor should respond within a few working days. If a verbal answer is not satisfactory, the employee can file the grievance in writing. Time limits should be brief, to require management to respond promptly. An employee should not be left hanging with no answer.

If the supervisor's answer does not settle the dispute, the employee should have the right to file the grievance with the personnel manager. After consultation with the department head, the personnel manager should provide the employee with the final management position in writing within three days.

At this point, an employee might have the option of appealing to the chief executive's office or submitting the case to impartial arbitration. The individual worker can arbitrate or use the open door. A request for arbitration should be filed promptly and delivered to the plant personnel office for processing.

The hearing would be held before an impartial arbitrator appointed by the American Arbitration Association. Other institutional sources for arbitrators appoint labor-management arbitrators who work within systems where a union is representing the employee. The jurisdiction of government agencies such as the Federal Mediation and Conciliation Service are restricted to labor management disputes.

The company may offer to provide a staff representative at no cost to the employee to help present the case before the arbitrator. Hearings can be held at a convenient location at the firm. Employees should not lose pay for the time spent in the arbitration hearing. No recordings or transcripts need to be made of the hearing. The arbitrator should be required to hand down a decision within a few working days after the hearing.

Among the grievances that can be arbitrated are wage rates, fringe benefits, job bidding, seniority rights, plant and safety rules, and other provisions covered in the employee handbook. If the company has agreed to discharge only for just cause, that issue can be arbitrated.

Employers who wish to offer their employees the option of arbitration should be sure that the system is essentially fair. The following points should be considered:

- The worker's use of arbitration should be voluntary. Employers who now provide access to the chief executive as the final step in the grievance procedure can offer employees the additional option of presenting their case to an impartial arbitrator appointed by an impartial agency. If the arbitrator is to be impartial, the selection should not be made by the employer.
- In some systems, the employee can select anyone to help present the case. Some employers may provide an acceptable representative from within the company. The employer must decide whether a grievant will have the right to be represented by an attorney, and if so, who will bear the cost. Employers should recognize that an attorney selected by a griev-

ant may be affiliated with a labor organization. An attorney who can demonstrate an ability to win cases, may be used by other grievants. If the employer decides not to permit grievants to be represented by attorneys of their coice, the finality of the award may be questionable. Some grievants may refuse to proceed without an attorney.

- The employer should pay all the expenses of the arbitration. Using expedited rules to eliminate the formalities, and exercising sensible cost control measures will reduce the cost. The arbitrator's per diem fee and an administrative fee may be the only outside costs.
- In some cases, the employer will agree in advance to be bound by the arbitrator's award, and may request the employee to give similar assurances. Whether such an award would be enforced by a court will depend on the facts of each case. Certainly, more weight will be given to the decision of an arbitrator than that of a company official.
- When arbitration is used for a termination case, the arbitrator might be limited to awarding compensation. The experience in Europe with such tribunals would indicate that most nonunion employees who have been unjustly discharged would prefer a cash settlement rather than being placed back on the job. It is one thing to reinstate a union member who can be represented by the shop steward. There is no such protection for the nonunion worker. In most situations it will be best to award appropriate severance pay, to be paid in exchange for a general release.

For employers wishing to install an informal system of arbitration, the following clause is recommended for inclusion in the employee manual:

An employee who is not satisfied with the decision of the Personnel Manager may request an arbitration hearing on the matter, under the Expedited Employment Rules of the American Arbitration Association. This recourse is available as an alternative to the final step in the internal procedure.

Other techniques and procedures are available that provide some independent review. An ombudsman, an official appointed by top management to investigate employee grievances, can be made a part of the corporate environment. The ombudsman generally reports directly to the chief executive and is outside the corporate chain of command. Major corporations identified with the use of an ombudsman have been Xerox, General Electric, and Boeing.

The ombudsman is an extension of the open door policy. If the chief executive had nothing else to do but solve personnel problems, he might serve as company ombudsman. In some smaller firms, the chief executive does exactly that. If anyone has a gripe, they go to the president.

In theory, the ombudsman is above the fray. In fact, the individual is identified with the authority of the chief executive. There are some problems. Employees hesitate to disclose their disputes to a chief executive. The intervention of top management in lower-level personnel decisions may strain the management structure. A president who becomes active in personnel problems may dislocate the delicate, personal relationships that an institution needs, undercut line relationships.

Mediation and fact finding are other third-party techniques. Mediation by management may translate into "working something out" or "making a deal." Fact finding is what the personnel director should do as soon as a problem surfaces.

The ombudsman, the open-door policy, mediation, and fact finding lack the credibility of impartial arbitration. The involvement of an outside neutral agency enhances credibility.

Worker Participation

To the extent that individual workers are given a greater voice in the production process, they may be better able to protect themselves. A working team can defend its individual members.

A new trend in American employment is to encourage employee participation at the production level. Companies such as General Motors, Ford, International Harvester, American Airlines, and Rockwell International have been involved in this movement. Some companies call these groups "quality circles." The American Productivity Center has encouraged the idea.

The members of the group are paid for their suggestions. For example, Northrop pays 10 percent for savings, both on the production line and in the office. Quality circles are intended to improve efficiency. They operate on the assumption that the people who do the work are most likely to know how to improve it. Usually, eight to ten workers are asked to serve on a circle. They meet with their immediate supervisor and a representative of the employee relations department.

After some preliminary fact gathering, the members of the circle focus on the problem, trying to develop ideas for saving time and money. Some spectacular savings have resulted. Quality circles "are part of a fundamental shift toward a new outlook on worker participation in decision making," according to one GM executive quoted in the *Wall Street Journal*.

That is the positive side. What of the worker whose job is lost as a result of the circle's recommendation? One group discovered a new way to keep rust from forming on the product. Unfortunately, one man's job was to brush off the rust as the product moved down the assembly line. The company gave him another job. What if no other job had been available?

What happens when a quality circle decides that a worker is incompetent or lazy? Fellow workers can be even more demanding than a supervisor but peer pressure may persuade some workers to shape up rather than drift into a position where they are subject to discharge.

Northrop also offers its nonunion employees a formal grievance procedure ending in arbitration. The procedure is available to every worker except supervisors. An employee who cannot settle a grievance with the supervisor can go directly to the Employee Relations office for an "impartial" investigation. A conference is held to "reach a mutually satisfactory adjustment." If no solution is reached, the employee may go on to a Management Appeals Committee, and then to arbitration. The arbitrator is chosen by the employee and the company by striking from a list. The decision of the arbitrator is binding upon both parties.

The Black Hole in the Law

Expanding the participation of individual employees in decision making may generate a demand for even greater due process. In *Freedom Inside the Organization—Bringing Civil Liberties to the Workplace,* David W. Ewing calls the present status a "black hole in American rights." He thinks that the rights of employees should be expanded, listing numerous examples of corporate injustice. He says that termination at will is inconsistent with modern society. "Most companies in the country are really totalitarian when you get down to it. All the freedom that people have on weekends and at night is blocked out completely when they get inside the company doors."

The Conference Board study shows that there is a trend to strengthen existing grievance procedures. Many of the new procedures include independent review. Some provide for arbitration, although the "open door" is more common.

In the long run, the continuing threat of unionization and the pressure of job-discrimination laws may persuade employers to go further. A fundamental change in the American system may be taking place. Nonunion employers may decide to submit just-cause questions to an impartial arbitrator, particularly if top executives find that the open-door policy is too time consuming.

David Ewing concedes that broader protection may not produce "magic increases in productivity and performance." He bases his argument on moral grounds. "It is time to begin erasing the division that afflicts some 85 million people and their families—totalitarianism at work versus freedom in the community."

To my mind, it is not so simple. Giving workers a new remedy does not necessarily cure the problem. It simply may place one organization in conflict with another. The employer, seeking to rid itself of an inefficient worker may find itself fighting with a government agency over its right to do so. If the government adopts narrow criteria, employers may be hamstrung. For the lack of a few selective discharges, massive layoffs may occur, as businessmen look elsewhere for more attractive yields.

I doubt that job security can be imposed by legislative mandate. Unless fundamental changes are made in our economic system, government cannot force investors to continue to employ people who are redundant. At the most, a more equitable system of termination payments might be imposed.

Ownership in the Job

Sometimes an imperceptible groundswell forecasts a massive social change. In an article in the *Wall Street Journal* on March 4, 1980, Peter F. Drucker pointed out that in other developed countries, as in America, the rights of the employee on the job seem to be evolving into a form of property. Drucker favors such job ownership because it will link the worker to the means of production. It may cure worker alienation.

To the extent that workers believe that they own part of the enterprise that employs them, their job may provide a greater sense of achievement and social status. With broadening participation in pension plans, employment provides continuing personal income earned as a result of job status. Recent laws have given pensions much of the protection reserved for property.

The idea that an employee owns his job may seem radical. We usually define property in terms of land, personal possessions, or income-producing securities. That a job can represent ownership requires some adjustment in our thinking but there is more to a job than a daily wage. For many of us, the compensation package includes many fringe benefits. The job is where we invest our time, our ego, and our hopes for the future. We become part of our job. Nine out of ten American workers are employed by organizations. The job provides status, personal opportunity, and power.

Drucker concludes that with the emergence of job property rights, employers must recognize that jobs cannot be taken away without due process. Firing, he says, must be subject to new rules. There must be a review procedure. Companies must develop objective standards of performance for all employees.

He believes that our emerging "employee society" is the most effective alternative to the "state capitalism" of the totalitarian governments, and points out that a similar trend is taking place in other countries. The mechanism differs, as we shall see, from culture to culture, but everywhere jobs are becoming a form of property.

With the exception of the handful of corporations that have pioneered in individual worker rights, management may resist the idea that workers own a property right in their jobs. Management needs to control the workforce to make the firm profitable and will zealously defend its right to terminate workers who don't contribute. This is true in profit-making firms which must respond to market pressures, and also in public and not-for-profit institutions where managers are expected to operate efficiently.

This traditional management attitude is devoutly held by most executives. It is shared by most employees and by the American public. It is unlikely that any description of hard-working and efficient Japanese or European workers will convince Americans otherwise. In any case, experience in other societies may not be relevant to the American problem.

American supervisors will continue to believe that their authority to fire inefficient workers is essential to good management. While recognizing that they must act within established rules and guidelines, they will defend their right to run the business.

Unionization has been resisted by management. Any proposal

for expanding employee rights that copies a system developed by organized labor will be suspect. Nonunion shop committees seeking to participate in the grievance process, besides presenting a danger of violating "company union" prohibitions, are too much like the traditional labor model. Arbitration is identified in many supervisors' minds with union pressure and may seem alien and threatening.

If job rights are regarded as property, employers may have to make changes in personnel practices. More care would have to be taken in hiring and in upgrading employees' skills. It may be more difficult to maintain flexibility in the assignment of human resources. If employers can't terminate nonproductive workers, they may be reluctant to seize new business opportunities. Staff reductions would have to be dealt with through attrition and alternative job-placement programs.

American industry must act quickly and decisively if it is to compete in the world market. Any change in the law that would inhibit management's flexibility could have harmful implications.

Management will resist any suggestion that its power be reduced. Even though many supervisors already believe that they must have a good reason for discharging an employee, management maintains control. Just cause does not have to be demonstrated to an outsider.

Many managers believe that the right to terminate a worker is essential in order to motivate workers to work faithfully and productively and that it should not become any more difficult than it already is to discharge an employee for unsatisfactory performance of duties.

Some people would disagree. Many employers already operate under a just-cause system. Unfair dismissals may reduce efficiency more than retaining a few questionable workers. When productive people are discharged for invalid reasons, the efficiency argument falls by the wayside. Unfair treatment may create a demoralized workforce.

When this issue was discussed at an annual meeting of the Industrial Relations Research Association in Atlanta, a representa-

tive of the AFL–CIO, Dick Wilson, warned that management
would stoutly defend its right to fire workers. Resistance from
management would be "total, without room for compromise."
He claimed that management was not so much concerned about
individual problems. More important, discharge is "often largely
symbolic in purpose. It is . . . used to keep the entire work force
in line." Termination at will, Wilson argues, is used to keep out
unions.

Counting the Votes on the Termination Issue

Whether or not it is true that employers use the threat of discharge to keep employees from organizing, it seems clear that employers will resist any suggestion that would abolish the termination-at-will doctrine because it gives them broad power to manage
their work force. As long as workers are willing to work under
such an arrangement, most employers will not change their approach.

The labor movement has seldom criticized the American system for discharging nonunion employees. Labor's victory against
unjust discharge occurred long ago when it won the right to protect union members. A worker represented by a union not only
has job security, backed up by a contractual remedy, but the National Labor Relations Act requires the union to represent him.
The union can force an employer to arbitrate.

An individual, nonunion worker would be in a different situation. An enlightened employer may promise to treat such a worker
with fairness, and may even agree to submit grievances to an impartial arbitrator. But the representation is lacking. The fairness
of the system depends upon the employer's continuing willingness
to maintain its original vision of employment justice. With increased use, such a system may become frustrating and expensive.
When the employer begins to lose cases, will it still want to arbitrate?

Perhaps enlightened corporations that create voluntary systems of grievance arbitration can be trusted to continue them. But there is no doubt that employees will require assistance in presenting cases. It will not be easy for the company to provide an equality of representation.

Employee protection is not free. Existing labor arbitration systems and civil-service hearing procedures are more costly than the internal grievance procedures now found in American nonunion companies. Even the industrial tribunals provided by the government in other countries can be costly.

Looking Abroad

The system in the United States is quite different than in other countries. If, in future years, our laws are amended, foreign labor laws may provide a model. Other countries provide termination compensation, with the cost fixed upon the employer. In most developed countries, an employee who is dismissed for any reason except fraud or dishonesty will be paid an indemnity. The amounts vary, depending upon the national law and applicable labor agreements. The employer's liability is based upon salary level, years of seniority, and the category of employment.

In some countries, payments are required even if the employee is terminated as a result of a plant closing, or if the employee resigns, becomes disabled, or retires. The termination allowance is considered a normal cost of doing business. In some countries, such as Venezuela, the employer must set aside funds during the active service of the worker.

Statutory termination indemnities can be substantial in some countries. Italy is generous in this regard. An employee dismissed with twenty years' service may receive thirty months of full salary. Usually, severance payments are paid only if an employee is dismissed without due cause. Austria and Italy are exceptions. In Austria, the payments are disbursed as a continued salary. In some countries, an additional amount is paid in lieu of notice of termination. For example, in Italy, twelve months' pay may be added to the already generous termination allowance if the employer fails to give adequate notice.

A review of labor laws in other countries shows that the United States has a unique system, relying primarily upon unemployment insurance to protect discharged workers. Throughout Europe, national laws provide direct protection against unjust dismissal. The French call it a principle of "stability of employment," meaning job security. This concept is not limited to Europe. Countries as varied as Algeria, Canada, Egypt, Japan, and Korea provide similar protection.

These employment-protection laws have some features in common. They apply to all employees who have completed a probationary period. They require the employer to give advance notice before dismissal, except in unusual cases. Most laws require the employer to pay money damages rather than to reinstate the employee. Usually, an employee is not free to quit without giving notice to the employer. Examples of some of the typical foreign laws follow.

England

Since 1971, British laws have provided comprehensive protection for employees who have been unfairly dismissed. The burden is on the employer to demonstrate the fairness of the dismissal. The legislation came as a result of the Donovan Commission report in 1968 and was intended to forestall strikes over individual dismissals, a chronic problem in the United Kingdom.

The individual rights provisions are contained in the Employment Protection Act. Complaints by employees must be first submitted to a government conciliation service, which disposes of more than a third of the cases. The conciliators not only try to settle the cases, they advise employers on how to improve their dismissal procedures.

According to Eileen Hoffman, who has studied that system, about 90 percent of the workload of the two hundred British conciliation officers is concerned with unfair dismissal complaints. Their work with the employer and the discharged worker is confidential, conducted mainly through separate meetings at which the conciliator tries to arrange a satisfactory settlement. A code of practice has been developed by the Advisory Conciliation and Arbitration Service which has been widely adopted by employers. It provides for prior warning, uniform disciplinary rules and an internal review procedure.

If the complaint is not settled, it must be presented to an industrial tribunal, a tripartite body made up of appointed officials. The chairman is a lawyer. These tribunals handle cases from more than a dozen labor laws; but four out of five cases concern unjust dismissals.

The determination as to whether a dismissal was fair depends on whether the employer can persuade the tribunal that the employer had a valid reason for dismissing the employee:

The tribunal may order reinstatement, but monetary awards are far more common. In calculating an appropriate award, the tribunal takes into account voluntary severance payments and unemployment benefits. The statute contains a formula for the basic award, to which is added something additional for the loss sustained in consequence of the dismissal. Thousands of cases are heard by such tribunals. About one-third of the dismissal cases result in decisions for the employee. Average awards are surprisingly low. For example, the median award in 1980 was $1,000.

The hearing itself is informal, similar to arbitration proceedings in the United States. Neither party is likely to be represented by an attorney. An average case will take about six months. Only a few cases are appealed although it is possible to take an appeal all the way to the House of Lords and litigation in the U.K. is notoriously expensive. Eileen Hoffman believes that the new procedure in Britain has sharply reduced the frequency of strikes over dismissals.

France

The system in France developed differently. Toward the end of the nineteenth century, French courts began to protect employees. Employers were held liable for terminating an employment contract if they acted with malicious intent, culpable negligence, or capriciousness.

In 1928, the abuse of right doctrine became part of the law. An employer could not discharge an employee for illness, for industrial injuries, pregnancy, political beliefs, exercising rights of citizenship, engaging in a strike, personal dislike, or if seniority procedures had not been followed.

After submitting the dispute to conciliation, an employee had the right to bring the employer to a labor court. The burden of proving an abuse of right is on the employee. The French labor courts lack authority to reinstate. Again, the usual remedy is compensation.

In practice, the French system is complicated. There are various kinds of reasons: light offenses which justify discharge; a grave offense "which makes it impossible to maintain the link of employment"; a heavy offense such as theft, bribery, and deliberate fraud which permits immediate action by the employer. These gradations are defined by court decisions. Each degree of justification is specified by the statutory law; the protection of employees can only be improved upon by contract.

In all aspects of employment, interaction takes place between workers, employers, work councils, union delegations, government commissions, and labor courts.

In France, a firm cannot reduce its work force without prior authorization from the government. If there are more than ten employees, the union must also be consulted.

Germany

In 1951, West Germany provided that a worker could be dismissed only if the action was "socially justified." The employer has the burden of proving the facts upon which the dismissal is based. The employer must show that it is not possible to keep the worker. As the law has been implemented by the German labor court, the reason for discharge must be job related. Dismissal must be necessary for effective operation of the business. The standard is similar but more demanding that the "just cause" requirement applicable to union contracts in the United States.

In 1972, the law was strengthened. Now a German employer must consult with the plant Work Council before giving notice of dismissal. The Work Council represents all of the workers, union and nonunion. Its importance in German labor relations cannot be understated. If the employer discharges a worker and the Work Council contradicts the decision, the employer must retain the employee until the case is decided. An employer will seldom risk a real conflict with the Work Council. Rather than try to prove justification for a discharge, employers will try to invent an economic reason for eliminating the position.

People from management and labor sit on the Labor Court, with a professional, lifetime judge. This is the case, not only at the first level, but also on the Court of Appeals. Conciliation is required before the case can come to hearing. If dissolution is sought by an employer, up to one year's salary may be awarded to the worker. Most cases are settled because the parties already know the likely result and face an extended period of litigation in the slow-moving German courts. Financial compensation is the normal result.

The German system puts great power into the hands of the local Work Council. This does not necessarily protect minority groups within the work force, such as women or ethnic minorities. Would America want to move in that direction?

Sweden

In 1974, Sweden enacted a law which provided that employment would be "until further notice," unless otherwise agreed. Dismissal can only be for "an objective cause," to be proven by the employer. Valid reasons for discharge include unexcused absence, insubordinaton, or negligence. The employer must consider not only the cause for dismissal but the employee's future usefulness. Dismissal without notice is allowed only for "serious neglect of duty."

An employee challenging a dismissal can sue in the Labor Court if he is a union member or in the regular courts if he is not. Most Swedish workers are unionized. If the dismissal is adjudged improper, it is declared invalid, but the courts cannot order reinstatement.

Japan

Japan's Labor Standard Law requires employers and unions to formulate rules of employment which define the occasions for which workers may be dismissed, to provide prior notice of the offense involved, and to provide procedural due process. These rules govern adjudication of discharge cases, particularly in the larger companies. In some ways, the review process in Japan resembles the arbitration process in this country, but, since it occurs in a culture that dislikes direct confrontations, the atmosphere at the hearing is more in the nature of a problem-solving conference.

The larger Japanese firms take responsibility for their permanent employees during their entire working careers, granting them substantially more job security than is customary in this country. This is done voluntarily, not because of legislative compulsion. Smaller firms often subcontract with the major corporations for particular services. With smaller firms, the workers may or may not have unions. These workers are less likely to have job security.

Mexico

Mexican labor law requires an employer to pay a termination indemnity to an employee whose employment has ended. There are two types of indemnity. The basic coverage is equal to three months' pay, plus twenty days' pay for each year of service. Thus, for an employee whose service is terminated after thirty-five years, the indemnity would equal about two years' earnings. The indemnity is not paid if the employee quits. If the employee is forced to retire, is fired, or is disabled, the employee is paid.

An additional seniority indemnity which is paid to employees with fifteen or more years of service is equal to twelve days' pay per year of covered service, but is limited to twice the minimum wage. That benefit is payable if the employee dies or is disabled or voluntarily retires or quits. Both indemnities are paid in a lump sum and are based on final pay.

Puerto Rico

The Puerto Rican labor law prohibits discharge "without good cause." Acceptable grounds for discharge are improper or disorderly conduct, repeated violations of the rules and regulations, failure to perform work efficiently, closing of the establishment, or layoffs because of reduction in production, sales, or profits.

Canada

In 1978, the Canada Labour Code was amended to afford protection against unjust dismissal for employees employed by Crown corporations, mainly banking, transportation, and communication workers. Under the new provisions, an adjudicator is authorized to provide protection for employees with more than one year seniority. Union members are not covered, nor are managers. First, the government provides a mediation process. Then, an adjudication is provided. The decisions have been based upon the principles developed under collective bargaining agreements. The decision is final and binding upon the parties, not subject to review in court. Up to March, 1980, 347 complaints had been received by Labour Canada. The provinces of Ontario, Nova Scotia, and Quebec are covered by similar provisions.

The ILO and European Community

The International Labour Organization in Geneva has attempted to create worldwide standards for handling employment terminations. They tend to follow the European model.

In 1960, after surveying its members, the ILO published Recommendation No. 119, *Concerning Termination of Employment at the Initiative of the Employer*. Termination should not take place unless there is a valid reason relating to the capacity or conduct of the worker, or based on the operational requirements of the undertaking. Union activity or filing a complaint against the employer for race, color, sex, marital status, religion, political opinion, national extraction, or social origin are not considered valid grounds for termination.

The ILO does not require that unjustly dismissed employees be reinstated, but states that the worker be entitled to compensation.

In 1976, the European Commission also attempted to bring uniformity to the laws of its member states. Dismissal should be limited to "serious grounds," where continuing employment is impossible or is unreasonable for economic or technical reasons, or because of the behavior of the worker. A worker who is incapable of doing the job may be fired. But dismissal should be the last resort and the employer must take into account a worker's age, length of service, future job prospects and family circumstances.

Some additional protection is recommended: consultation with worker representatives should precede dismissal; the worker should be given written notice of at least thirty days, except where summary dismissal is necessary; and the legality of the dismissal should be examined by an independent body.

Should the U.S. Copy Foreign Systems?

The employment climate in Europe is substantially different than ours. In the United States, a much smaller percentage of workers are members of unions, less than 25 percent. Many American workers do not commit themselves to permanent career positions to the extent that Europeans do. We place a high value upon our right to switch jobs and to move freely within the employment market. In Europe, a worker is expected to give notice of an intention to change jobs. The Common Market standards may not be appropriate for our culture.

Our system may be best suited for our particular society because it encourages diversity. Workers who believe that they need the protection of a union can vote to be represented under the provisions of the National Labor Relations Law. As union members, they will be protected against being dismissed without just cause. The union will represent them in arbitration, as it is required to do.

Employees who elect not to be represented by a union may deal directly with the employer. If they are discharged, they must represent their own interests. If they can't persuade the employer to reconsider the termination, they can accept the discharge and apply for unemployment insurance benefits. Or they can retain a lawyer to contest the discharge in court under whatever theory of law may fit a particualr protective statues.

Many of the examples in this book illustrate cases where employees felt that they should not have been discharged. They are not intended to demonstrate massive corporate injustice. They do indicate how difficult it is to weigh individual rights against the firm's economic interests. They raise important questions about the American workplace. Should corporations have an unlimited right to fire employees? How much due process in employment can we afford? What is the best way to protect people from losing their jobs?

If change is desired by the American people, change will occur. An increasing number of firms may become unionized. Congress may strengthen the legal rights of employees. Courts may enlarge upon the doctrines of unjust dismissal or implied contract. We may copy systems existing in other countries. Or we may not.

It is important that Americans think about these issues. Most of us invest much of our lives in our work. Our rights as employees are important because the job is such a major part of our lives. How we feel about our work may determine how we feel about society, about ourselves. We live in a free country. If we do not feel free when are are at work, our alienation may be transmitted into our attitudes about other institutions.

America must increase its productivity. Our standard of living and our ability to afford the many freedoms that this country provides will depend upon our material prosperity. In America the balance between individual and organization has been set in various ways. Even within the present legal parameters, that balance depends upon the views of management and the desires of the people working in each organization. Some employers are harsh and autocratic: others are known to be fair.

The Conference Board report on Nonunion Complaint Systems indicates a growing recognition by American industry that it may be good business to create internal methods for recognizing "problems where and when they arise, and to resolve them within the company." Whether the motivation is to avoid legal issues or to insure that company policy will be followed or to deal with conflicts in personality, many employers have concluded that employee grievances should be resolved fairly and with dispatch.

If there is increasing unhappiness with a lack of fairness in the workplace, as some observers indicate, farsighted managers seem willing to create new mechanisms for dealing with these problems. The Conference Board concluded that one motivation has been to freeze out unions. My own view, to the contrary, is that management is responding to the personal needs of employees. Americans prefer fair treatment. They are seeking it at work as they seek it elsewhere in society.

A young typist at the American Arbitration Association put it very well, "My supervisor gives me more work than she gives the other girls. When I complain, she tells me to shut up and do the work. I wouldn't talk that way. Why should she?"

At first, these policy questions seem easy to answer: Should employers be required to treat their employees with fairness? Of course. Should employers be required to justify a decision to discharge an employee? Why not? It is easy to answer in the affirmative: but what will it cost?

The rules of the workplace seem to be in flux. Some employers are voluntarily adopting restraints upon their right to discharge. Others continue to treat their employees as an expendable resource, discharging them whenever they decide to do so.

If too many unfair incidents take place, the public will be persuaded that there is a need to reform the employment law. State and federal courts may abandon the termination-at-will doctrine, giving workers the right to test the reasons for their discharge, making it more difficult for employers to terminate unsatisfactory employees. Statutory changes could achieve the same goal.

The vitality of our economic system requires that managers have the discretion to make efficient use of human resources. Decisions to invest in plants and in people are made in a competitive marketplace, and increasingly in an international marketplace. In order to pursue shifting advantages, investors must be able to respond flexibly and quickly.

Our national policies have favored programs that sustain family income while permitting job change and shifts in employment. We have encouraged mobility rather than attempting to stabilize workers in one job for life. We have aspired to be a free society.

Proposals to abandon that ideal by imposing further restrictions on employer rights will meet strenuous objections from management. Through the long history of human endeavor, there have been few instances where powerful interests have abandoned their right to make unilateral decisions. In Connecticut and other states where legislation has been proposed to eliminate management's discretion to discharge workers, business has lobbied against it. Management resistance will not evaporate even if public attitudes change.

There are practical reasons why an employer wants to maintain control over the workforce. In spite of a new emphasis upon employee participation and better working conditions, the threat of discharge is a valued weapon in the management arsenal. Pressures transmitted through management to the supervisor are intense. Profits depend upon an efficient operation. Management will want to discharge employees who lack the desire or ability to do the work. Whether our system changes or stays the same, the employment relationship will always involve conflict. As workers and supervisors wrangle over their differences, dismissals will continue to occur. Management will have to deal with such problems.

Posterity will determine whether or not decisions to discharge workers will be reviewed internally, will be decided by private arbitrators or will be taken to government tribunals or to the courts. Trying to forecast that event is not the purpose of this book. Our aim here has been to provide information for individuals involved in the termination process, to help avoid unnecessary litigation, needless cruelty, and mindless confusion.

By understanding the system under which workers are fired, you can play an intelligent and humane role when you become involved in a firing. Try to understand what pressures are making the other person say what must be said. Learn to think in terms of finding a mutually acceptable solution. In a free society, we must try to be brothers, helping each other to find our way through life.

American Arbitration Association Expedited Employment Arbitration Rules

1. Agreement of Parties—These Rules shall apply whenever the parties have agreed to arbitrate under them, in the form obtaining at the time the arbitration is initiated.

2. Appointment of Neutral Arbitrator—The AAA shall appoint a single neutral Arbitrator from its Panel of Arbitrators, who shall hear and determine the case promptly.

3. Initiation of Expedited Arbitration Proceeding—Cases may be initiated by joint submission in writing or in accordance with a prior agreement.

4. Qualification of Neutral Arbitrator—No person shall serve as a neutral Arbitrator in any arbitration in which that person has any financial or personal interest in the result of the arbitration. Prior to accepting an appointment, the prospective Arbitrator shall disclose any circumstances likely to prevent a prompt hearing or to create a presumption of bias. Upon receipt of such information, the AAA shall immediately replace that Arbitrator or communicate the information to the parties.

5. Vacancy—The AAA is authorized to substitute another

Arbitrator if a vacancy occurs or if an appointed Arbitrator is unable to serve promptly.

6. Time and Place of Hearing—The Arbitrator shall fix the time and place for the hearing, notice of which must be given at least 24 hours in advance, unless the parties otherwise agree. Such notice may be given orally, in person or by telephone.

7. Representation—Any party may represent itself or be represented by any person it designates.

8. Attendance at Hearings—Persons having a direct interest in the arbitration are entitled to attend hearings. The Arbitrator may require the retirement of any witness during the testimony of other witnesses. The Arbitrator shall determine whether any other person may attend the hearing.

9. Adjournments—Hearings shall be adjourned by the Arbitrator only for good cause, and an appropriate fee will be charged by the AAA against the party causing the adjournment.

10. Oaths—Before proceeding with the first hearing, the Arbitrator shall take an oath of office. The Arbitrator may require witnesses to testify under oath.

11. No Stenographic Record—There shall be no stenographic record of the proceedings.

12. Proceedings—The hearing shall be conducted by the Arbitrator in whatever manner will most expeditiously permit full presentation of the evidence and arguments of the parties. Normally, the hearing shall be completed within one day. In unusual circumstances and for good cause shown, the Arbitrator may schedule an additional hearing, within five days.

13. Arbitration in the Absence of a Party—The arbitration may proceed in the absence of any party who, after due notice, fails to be present. An award shall not be made solely on the default of a party. The Arbitrator shall require the attending party to submit supporting evidence.

14. Evidence—The Arbitrator shall be the sole judge of the relevancy and materiality of the evidence offered.

15. Evidence by Affidavit and Filing of Documents—The Arbitrator may receive and consider evidence in the form of an affidavit, but shall give appropriate weight to any objections made.

All documents to be considered by the Arbitrator shall be filed at the hearing. There shall be no post hearing briefs.

16. Close of Hearings—The Arbitrator shall ask whether parties have any further proofs to offer or witnesses to be heard. Upon receiving negative replies, the Arbitrator shall declare and note the hearing closed.

17. Waiver of Rules—Any party who proceeds with the arbitration after knowledge that any provision or requirement of these Rules has not been complied with and who fails to state objections thereto in writing shall be deemed to have waived the right to object.

18. Serving of Notices—Any papers or process necessary or proper for the initiation or continuation of an arbitration under these Rules and for any court action in connection therewith or for the entry of judgment on an award made thereunder, may be served upon such party (a) by mail addressed to such party or its attorney at its last known address, or (b) by personal service, or (c) as otherwise provided in these Rules.

19. Time of Award—The award shall be rendered promptly by the Arbitrator and, unless otherwise agreed by the parties, not later than five business days from the date of the closing of the hearing.

20. Form of Award—The award shall be in writing and shall be signed by the Arbitrator. If the Arbitrator determines that an opinion is necessary, it shall be in summary form.

21. Delivery of Award to Parties—Parties shall accept as legal delivery of the award the placing of the award or a true copy thereof in the mail by the AAA, addressed to such party at its last known address or to its attorney, or personal service of the award, or the filing of the award in any manner which may be prescribed by law.

22. Expenses—The expenses of witnesses for either side shall be paid by the party producing such witnesses.

23. Interpretation and Application of Rules—The Arbitrator shall interpret and apply these Rules insofar as they relate to the Arbitrator's powers and duties. All other Rules shall be interpreted and applied by the AAA, as Administrator.

Selected Bibliography

BERENBEIM, RONALD. *Nonunion Complaint Systems: A Corporate Appraisal.* Report no. 770. New York: The Conference Board, 1980.

BLACKBURN, JOHN D. "Restricted Employer Discharge Rights: A Changing Concept of Employment at Will." *American Business Law Journal,* vol. 17 (Winter 1980), pp. 467–492.

BLADES, LAWRENCE E. "Employment at Will vs. Individual Freedom: On Limiting the Abusive Exercise of Employer Power." *Columbia Law Review,* vol. 67, no. 8 (December 1967), pp. 1404–1435.

BLUMROSEN, ALFRED W. "Strangers No More: All Workers Are Entitled to Just Cause Protection Under Title VII." *Industrial Relations Law Journal,* vol. 2 (1978), p. 519.

CHIPMAN, LESTER D. "Proper Grievance Handling Makes Unions Unnecessary." *Civil Engineering* (September 1973), pp. 95–97.

COULSON, ROBERT. "Arbitration for the Individual Employee." *Employee Relations Law Journal,* vol. 5, no. 3 (Winter 1979–80), pp. 406–415.

——. "Employment Dispute Arbitration Rules—An Available Alternative." In Southwestern Legal Foundation, *Proceedings of Twenty-Fifth Annual Institute on Labor Law, October 4–5, 1978, Dallas, Texas,* pp. 311–334. New York: Matthew Bender, 1979.

——. *How to Arbitrate the Employment Rights Claims of Individual Employees.* Englewood Cliffs, N.J.: Prentice-Hall, 1979.

——. "Impartial Review: A New Fringe Benefit." Remarks Presented at the Civil Liberties Review, Second National Seminar on Individual Rights in the Corporation, June 25, 1979. New York: American Arbitration Association, 1979. Also Published in *Daily Labor Report,* no. 123 (June 25, 1979), pp. D-1–D-2.

———. "New Fringe Benefit: Voluntary Arbitration of Job-Rights Claims." *New York Law Journal* (April 13, 1978), p. 1.

———. "Rising Expectations for Job Security in Corporate America." *New York Law Journal* (January 1, 1980), p. 1.

"Dealing with White Collar Gripes." *Personnel Administrator,* October 1978, pp. 34–35.

"Disciplinary Practice and Procedures in Employment." *Code of Practice* 1. London. Advisory Conciliation and Arbitration Service, 1977.

DROUGHT, NEAL E. "Grievances in the Nonunion Situation." *Personnel Journal,* vol. 46, no. 6 (June 1967), pp. 331–336.

"Employee Complaints Get Fair Hearing from Xerox Ombudsman." *Employee Relations Bulletin* (August 7, 1974), p. 1.

"Employment at Will—Limitations on Employer's Freedom to Terminate." *Louisiana Law Review,* vol. 35, no. 3 (Spring 1975), pp. 710–715.

EPSTEIN, RICHARD L. "The Grievance Procedure in the Non-union Setting: Caveat Employer." *Employee Relations Law Journal,* vol. 1, no. 1 (Spring 1975), pp. 120–127.

"Evaluation of a Grievance Procedure for Non-union Employees." *What's Ahead in Personnel* (September 30, 1979), pp. 1–4.

EWING, DAVID W. *Freedom Inside the Organization: Bringing Civil Liberties to the Workplace.* New York: E.P. Dutton, 1977.

FOULKES, FRED K. *Personnel Policies in Large Non-union Companies.* Englewood Cliffs, N.J.: Prentice-Hall, 1981.

FOWLER, ELIZABETH M. "New Field: Workers' Grievances." *New York Times,* February 13, 1980.

GETMAN, JULIUS G. "Labor Arbitration and Dispute Resolution." *Yale Law Journal,* vol. 88 (1979), pp. 916–948.

HARRIS, DAVID. "Wrongful Dismissal—Some Recent Developments." *Advocates Quarterly,* vol. 2 (January 1980), pp. 149–152.

HEPPLE, B.A. "Community Measures for the Protection of Workers Against Dismissal." *Common Market Law Review,* vol. 14 (1977), pp. 489–500.

HERMAN, SIDNEY. "Faculty Grievance Procedures in a Non-union Context." In National Center for the Study of Collective Bargaining in Higher Education, *Collective Bargaining in Higher Education: Proceedings, Fourth Annual Conference, April 1976,* pp. 28–35. New York: Baruch College–CUNY, n.d.

HOLLOWAY, WILLIAM J. "Fired Employees Challenging Terminable-at-Will Doctrine." *National Law Journal,* vol. 1, no. 23 (February 19, 1979), p. 22.

HOWLETT, G. "Due Process for Nonunionized Employees. A Practical Proposal." *IRRA 32nd Annual Proceedings* (1980), pp. 164–170.

"How to Take the Grief Out of Grievances." *Employee Relations Bulletin* (Baltimore Gas and Electric Company) (June 21, 1977), pp. 6–7.

JOHNSON, JUDITH J. "Protected Concerted Activity in the Non-union Context: Limitations on the Employer's Rights to Discipline or Discharge Employees." *Mississippi Law Journal,* vol. 49, no. 2 (December 1978), pp. 839–880.

KILGOUR, JOHN G. "Before the Union Knocks." Part I. *Personnel Journal,* vol. 57, no. 4 (April 1978), p. 186.

LEHAIN, P. "Calculating the Quantum of Damages for Wrongful Dismissal." *New Law Journal,* vol. 129 (September 6, 1979), pp. 882–890.

"Listening and Responding to Employees' Concerns: An Interview with A.W. Clausen." *Harvard Business Review,* vol. 58, no. 1 (January/February 1980), pp. 101–114.

MADISON, JAMES R. "The Employee's Emerging Right to Sue for Arbitrary or Unfair Discharge." *Employee Relations Law Journal,* vol. 6, no. 3 (Winter 1980), pp. 422–436.

MICHAEL, STEPHEN R. "Due Process in Nonunion Grievance Systems." *Employee Relations Law Journal,* vol. 3, no. 4 (Spring 1978), pp. 516–527.

MOONEY, T.B., AND J.C. PINGPANK. "Wrongful Discharge: A 'New' Cause of Action?" *Connecticut Bar Journal,* vol. 54 (June 1980), pp. 213–234.

NATIONAL ASSOCIATION OF MANUFACTURERS. Industrial Relations Division. *Settling Complaints in the Non-unionized Operation.* Information Bulletin no. 26. New York: 1957.

PECK, C. J. "Some Kind of Hearing for Persons Discharged from Private Employment." *San Diego Law Review,* vol. 16, no. 2 (March 1979), pp. 313–324.

———. "Unjust Discharges from Employment: A Necessary Change in Law." *Ohio State Law Journal,* vol. 40 (1979), pp. 1–49.

PERSONNEL POLICIES FORUM. *Personnel Policies for Unorganized Employees.* Survey no. 84. Washington, D.C.: Bureau of National Affairs, 1968.

———. *Policies for Unorganized Employees.* Survey no. 125. Washington, D.C.: Bureau of National Affairs, 1979.

"Protecting at Will Employees against Wrongful Discharge: The Duty to Terminate Only in Good Faith." *Harvard Law Review,* vol. 93, no. 8 (June 1980), pp. 1816–1844.

"Recognizing the Employees' Interests in Continued Employment—The California Cause of Action for Unjust Dismissal." *Pacific Law Journal,* vol. 12 (October 1980), pp. 69–96.

ROBERTS, JOHN C. "Termination Indemnities Around the World." *The Personnel Administrator* (June 1979).

STREIBER, JACK. "Protection Against Unfair Dismissal." *Industrial Relations Newsletter* (Fall 1978), p. 4.

SUMMERS, CLYDE W. "Individual Protection Against Unjust Dismissal: Time for a Statute." *Virginia Law Review,* vol. 62, no. 3 (April 1976), pp. 481–532.

———. "Protecting All Employees Against Unjust Dismissal." *Harvard Business Review,* vol. 58, no. 1 (January/February 1980), pp. 132–139.

TRANS WORLD AIRLINES. *Noncontract Employee Grievance Procedure.* New York: 1973.

"Unjust Dismissal. Letters to the Editor." *Harvard Business Review,* vol. 58, no. 2 (March/April 1980), p. 66.

URIS, AJREN. *Executive Dissent.* New York: AMACOM, 1978.

VERNON, RICHARD G., AND PETER S. GRAY. "Termination at Will—The Employers' Right to Fire." *Employee Relations Law Journal,* vol. 6, no. 1 (Summer 1980), pp. 25–40.

WARREN, WILLIAM H. "Ombudsman Plus Arbitration: A Proposal for Effective Grievance Administration Without Public Employee Unions." *Labor Law Journal,* vol. 29, no. 9 (September 1978), pp. 562–569.

WESTIN, ALAN F., AND STEPHEN SALISBURY. *Individual Rights in the Corporation: A Reader on Employee Rights.* New York: Pantheon, 1980.

WILLIAMS, K. "Job Security and Unfair Dismissal." *Modern Law Review,* vol. 38 (May 1975), pp. 292–310.

YENNEY, SHARON L. "In Defense of the Grievance Procedure in a Nonunion Setting." *Employee Relations Law Journal,* vol. 2, no. 4 (Spring 1977), pp. 434–443.

Index

229